PRAISE FOR MICHAEL HACKARD

"As a trust and estate litigator and partner at Trust Law Partners, I've spent over two decades navigating complex inheritance disputes. Yet Michael Hackard's 'Inheritance Heists' offers fresh insights even for seasoned practitioners. Drawing from five decades in the field, Hackard masterfully dissects contemporary challenges - from caregiver exploitation to cryptocurrency theft - while providing practical solutions. His innovative analysis of contingency fee arrangements is particularly valuable. What sets this work apart is Hackard's deep understanding of both the legal and emotional dynamics of inheritance disputes. An essential resource for anyone practicing in California's estate litigation landscape."

Jeff Loew, Partner, Trust Law Partners, California

"I serve the court in matters of estate and civil litigation when acts of fraud, waste, and undue influence are so egregious it rises to the necessity to have an independent fiduciary take full possession and control of assets, including real property, investment accounts, and businesses. My role is sometimes referred to as the "nuclear option" to protect and preserve the Estate until the litigation is resolved. In my world, everything that can go wrong does go wrong. That is why I implore people to take notice and learn from the real examples and exceptionally knowledgeable advice Mike shares in this book. I have worked with Mike on litigation matters over the years and what I most appreciate is Hackard Law offers people who cannot afford to hire legal services an opportunity to pursue their equitable rights to receive what was denied to them by bad actors with skilled and effective practices in law."

Daniel Collins, Court Appointed Receiver, Collins Commercial

"For anyone planning to leave a legacy to their loved ones, *Inheritance Heists* is indispensable. Hackard brings decades of estate law expertise to two critical areas: preventing family disputes before they arise and resolving conflicts when estate assets are mishandled or misappropriated. Dealing with disputing estate beneficiaries about what they should receive, according to the terms of the legal documents, requires careful legal consideration. Through clear guidance and practical insights, he demonstrates why careful estate planning is crucial for ensuring your final wishes are honored. The book serves as both a preventive guide and a practical resource, helping readers anticipate potential conflicts while providing legal solutions when problems arise. Whether you're planning your estate or dealing with inheritance issues, Hackard's balanced perspective on both preventive measures and conflict resolution makes this an invaluable resource for protecting your family's legacy."

Brad Parker, President, Texas Trial Lawyers Association (2013)

"As a law firm growth strategist who has dedicated her career to helping attorneys transform their practices, I recognize in Michael Hackard's *Inheritance Heists* a masterful blueprint that mirrors the core principles of systematic, principled, professional growth. Just as my work at KerriJames focuses on building predictable, data-driven systems for law firms, Hackard demonstrates an equally methodical approach to estate litigation - transforming complex legal challenges into strategic, ethical advocacy.

Hackard's contingency fee model, which grants access to all who seek justice, perfectly embodies the kind of innovative thinking I champion. By removing financial barriers and aligning attorney interests with client needs, he does precisely what I teach law firms: create systems that serve both professional excellence and human dignity."

Kerri Coby White, Founder, KerriJames;
Author, *The Law Firm Growth Machine*

"*Inheritance Heists* by Michael Hackard explores the complex world of estate and trust litigation. The book reveals how family legacies can be undermined by manipulation, undue influence, and deception. Hackard, a veteran attorney, uses real-world case studies to expose inheritance challenges, including trust distribution disasters, caregiver exploitation, and family conflicts. The book introduces Hackard Law's innovative contingency fee model, which expands access to justice for families fighting inheritance injustices. By examining biblical principles of truthfulness and ethical behavior, Hackard provides practical strategies to families and professionals for preventing and resolving inheritance disputes, emphasizing the importance of communication, transparency, and protecting family legacies. As an example, I have seen the calming effect I can bring to contentious family dynamics because I am an independent third party fiduciary with no involvement in the family history or drama."

John DePiazza, Fiduciary, AD Fiduciary

"Drawing from over three decades of experience advising high-net-worth clients and serving as an expert witness in securities cases, I can attest that Michael Hackard's *Inheritance Heists* is an essential resource for financial advisors and estate planning professionals. His practical insights on preventing inheritance fraud, particularly in cases involving digital assets and blended families, align perfectly with the systematic and accountable approach we champion at Lighthouse Strategic Advisors. This book is a valuable tool for protecting clients' legacies."

Dave Siegel, Senior Partner, Lighthouse Strategic Advisors, West Point Graduate, and Former Army Ranger

INHERITANCE HEISTS

RECLAIM YOUR FAMILY'S LEGACY AND FIGHT
BACK AGAINST FINANCIAL PREDATORS

MICHAEL HACKARD

HACKARD GLOBAL MEDIA

Copyright © 2025 by Michael Hackard

All rights reserved.

No part of this book may be reproduced in any form or by any electronic or mechanical means, including information storage and retrieval systems, without written permission from the author, except for the use of brief quotations in a book review.

All materials, stories, law, and conclusions contained in this book are for general information only. The information in this book is not legal advice, should not be relied upon as legal advice, may not be current, and is subject to change without notice.

Publisher's Cataloging-In-Publication Data

Title: Inheritance heists / Michael Hackard.

Description: [First edition]. | [Sacramento, California] : Hackard Global Media, [2025] | Subtitle on cover: Reclaim your family's legacy and fight back against financial predators.

Identifiers: ISBN: 978-0-9991446-9-5 (paperback) | 978-0-9991446-8-8 (ebook)

Subjects: LCSH: Inheritance and succession--United States--Popular works. | Wills--United States-- Popular works. | Estate planning--United States--Popular works. | Claims against decedents' estates--United States. | Finance, Personal--United States. | Financial security-- United States. | Older people--Legal status, laws, etc.--United States. | Legal assistance to older people-- United States. | Dementia--Patients--Legal status, laws, etc.--United States. | Stepfamilies-- Legal status, laws, etc.--United States. | Stepchildren-- Legal status, laws, etc.--United States. | Data protection--Law and legislation--United States. | Digital rights management--United States.

Classification: LCC: KF753 .H33 2025 | DDC: 346.7305/2--dc23

Hackard Global Media, LLC

10630 Mather Blvd.

Mather, CA 95655-4125

Printed in the United States of America

To My Beloved Grandchildren,

As I wrap up this book about inheritance and family legacies, I'm thinking about you - the incredible next chapter of our family's story.

You're so much more than potential inheritors of some legal document or financial assets. You're the living, breathing continuation of everything our family stands for. My hope is that this book becomes more than just legal guidance - it's a love letter to our family's resilience, faith, integrity, and unbreakable bonds.

"Grandchildren are the crown of the aged," and all of you are my crown. Each of you represents not just a branch on our family tree, but a vibrant promise of everything we've built together. May you see your own children's children, carrying forward the legacy of love, courage, and connection that defines us.

This book isn't about money. It's about something far more precious – the faith in our God, the values we pass down, the stories we share, and the relationships we nurture. Remember that your truest inheritance isn't found in a trust or will, but in the lessons, love, and memories we create together.

With all my heart and hope for your futures,

Boompa

CONTENTS

Preface: Why I Write ... xi
Introduction: Stopping Inheritance Heists ... xiii

PART ONE

1. When Good Intentions Go Awry: Trust Distribution Disasters ... 3
2. Adapting the Blueprint: When Life Outpaces Estate Plans ... 17
3. No Win, No Fee: How Contingency Arrangements Transform Estate Litigation ... 24
4. The Emotional Landscape of Inheritance Disputes ... 35
5. The Truth About Lies: When Deception Taints Inheritance ... 42
6. The Presumption of Fraud: When the Law Suspects Foul Play ... 53
7. Mastering Mediation Negotiation: The Art of Resolving Inheritance Disputes ... 58

PART TWO

8. From Hospital Bed to Mediation Room: Resolving Inheritance Conflicts ... 75
9. Caregiver Capers: When Trust Turns to Treachery ... 81
10. The Digital Frontier: Navigating Cryptocurrency Litigation and Estate Planning ... 95
11. Blended Families and Inheritance: Balancing Competing Interests ... 104
12. When Trust Breaks Down: Navigating Stepparent Inheritance Conflicts ... 113
13. Safeguarding Legacies and Championing Justice ... 118

Glossary of Terms ... 127
Index ... 135
About the Author ... 147
Also by Michael Hackard ... 149

PREFACE: WHY I WRITE

At the time of writing this preface, my home state of California is being ravaged by wildfires – from Pacific Palisades to Pasadena, the headlines are ominous. Several people have died, thousands of homes and businesses are in ruins, and estimates of the damage now exceed $100 billion.

A tragedy of this scale affects countless families in the most visible and painful of ways. I'll leave it to experts to determine the extent to which natural disasters like this are preventable. A collective tragedy caused by an act of nature may not have a direct culprit – but the individual tragedy of the inheritance heist usually does. And for a family whose inheritance is stolen, the devastation – both material and emotional - is comparable. The childhood home gone, assets vaporized, an entire legacy and hope for the future destroyed.

I'm writing to help you, the reader, avoid inheritance disaster. There are "red flags" – distinct warning signals of estate or trust wrongdoing – that you can detect and follow up with preventive measures. You can stop the financial exploitation of an elderly loved one if you spot it early enough, and you can safeguard an estate as its rightful heir.

Other readers may be victims of an inheritance heist – a wrongdoer, whether it's another family member or an interloper, has managed to hijack their family's estate or trust. I write for you as well. The sting of loss of a loved one is compounded by the injustice of a stolen legacy. You, too, can take legal action to reclaim your inheritance, but you'll need to prepare for a tough fight ahead.

I tell my clients who have been wrongfully disinherited or excluded from a trust a simple truth: "We're starting at zero." You may be facing an uphill battle, but with an experienced estate litigator on your side, you can even the odds and reach a better outcome. Financial recovery through our court system may be relatively simple compared to what every client must still face: shattered trust, emotional trauma, and families divided. None of this is easy.

Yet my motivation in writing *Inheritance Heists* is to share a message of hope through practical guidance. Lies and fraud succeed only under cover of night, and it's my mission to shine a powerful spotlight on estate thieves. Ephesians 5:11 counsels us: "Have nothing to do with the fruitless deeds of darkness, but rather expose them." Be courageous and take heart.

INTRODUCTION: STOPPING INHERITANCE HEISTS

In the twilight of a person's life, as families grapple with loss and transition, a silent predator often lurks in the shadows: the inheritance heist. This insidious form of financial exploitation preys on the vulnerable, capitalizing on grief, confusion, and family discord to divert assets away from their rightful heirs.

As a veteran attorney with nearly five decades of experience, I've witnessed firsthand the devastating impact these schemes can have on families and estates. I founded Hackard Law, one of California's leading contingency fee estate and trust litigation law firms, to battle more than just these legal violations. These acts represent profound breaches of moral responsibility and human dignity.

This book serves three distinct but interconnected audiences. First and foremost, it's written for families who want to protect their legacies and avoid becoming victims of inheritance heists. Whether you're creating an estate plan, helping an aging parent manage their affairs, or simply want to understand the risks and warning signs, this book provides crucial preventive strategies and practical guidance.

Second, it's for those already embroiled in inheritance disputes - the children cut out of their parents' will, the siblings facing a trust distribution disaster, or the elderly struggling with caregiver exploitation. If you're fighting to recover your rightful inheritance, you'll find both tactical advice and the emotional support needed to navigate these challenging waters.

Finally, this book serves as an essential resource for legal professionals, financial advisors, and other practitioners who guide families through these complex situations. By understanding both the technical and human elements of inheritance disputes, these professionals can better serve their clients and prevent costly conflicts before they arise. Whether you're planning for the future, fighting a current battle, or advising others, this book offers the insights and strategies needed to stop inheritance heists and protect family legacies.

THE NATURE OF INHERITANCE HEISTS

An *inheritance heist*, in its simplest terms, is the unlawful or unethical appropriation of assets intended for rightful heirs. These heists can take many forms, from the subtle manipulation of a vulnerable elder to alter his or her will, to the outright theft of assets by unscrupulous executors or trustees. The methods may vary, but the result is always the same: a betrayal of the deceased's wishes and a profound injustice to the intended beneficiaries. This betrayal undermines not only legal standards but also the essential values that support human well-being and the collective good.

One particularly troubling form of inheritance heist involves trust distribution disasters. These occur when carefully laid plans for asset distribution through trusts go awry, often due to unclear language, unequal distributions, timing issues, or trustee mismanagement. Such disasters can lead to protracted legal battles, eroded estate values, and irreparably damaged family relationships.

The perpetrators of these heists are not always strangers. In fact, they are often family members, trusted advisors, or caregivers who exploit their position of trust. The culprit may use undue influence, forgery, or even outright fraud to redirect assets to themselves or others. The emotional and financial toll on families can be immense, often tearing apart relationships and leaving lasting scars.

Another troubling form of inheritance heist involves caregiver exploitation. As we'll explore in depth, caregivers - whether family members or professionals - can sometimes abuse a position of trust to manipulate vulnerable elders and redirect assets for personal gain.

These heists, in their many forms, require a different kind of legal response than traditional probate practice typically provides. The stakes are too high and the perpetrators too bold for business as usual.

A GROWING PROBLEM

Since litigating my first inheritance heist case shortly after becoming an attorney in 1976, I've seen these scenarios play out time and time again. At Hackard Law, we handle dozens of such cases each year throughout California, from Sacramento to Los Angeles and San Francisco to San Jose. Our approach has always been to look beyond mere legal technicalities to consider the broader purpose of our actions and advice, recognizing that our role as attorneys extends beyond technical competence to serving the common good. The frequency and complexity of these disputes have only increased over time, mirroring the growing wealth of the aging population and the evolving dynamics of modern families.

Several factors contribute to this troubling trend:

An aging population: As the Baby Boomer generation enters their twilight years, we're seeing an unprecedented transfer of wealth. This creates more opportunities for unscrupulous individuals to take advantage of vulnerable elders.

Complex family structures: With blended families becoming more common, the potential for conflicts over inheritance has increased. Stepchildren, half-siblings, and multiple marriages can complicate the distribution of assets.

Digital assets: The rise of digital assets, from cryptocurrency to online accounts, has created new challenges in estate planning and new avenues for theft. As we'll explore in Chapter 5, these digital fortunes can be particularly vulnerable to theft and mismanagement if proper precautions aren't taken. Elders' retirement nest eggs can be swept away in an electronic heartbeat.

Increased longevity: As people live longer, there's a higher risk of cognitive decline, making them more susceptible to manipulation and undue influence.

Increased reliance on caregivers: As the population ages and more seniors require daily assistance, the number of caregiving relationships has increased. While most caregivers are dedicated and ethical, this trend has unfortunately also created more opportunities for exploitation.

Changing family dynamics: With the clash of more complex family structures and an increased reliance on caregivers, the potential for conflicts and exploitation in inheritance matters has grown significantly.

Stepparent dynamics: With the increase in blended families, conflicts between stepparents and biological children over inheritance have become more prevalent. These situations often involve complex emotional dynamics and can be particularly prone to inheritance disputes.

THE IMPACT OF INHERITANCE HEISTS

The consequences of these heists extend far beyond the financial realm. They represent a violation of both legal and moral principles that can:

- Destroy family relationships, often irreparably,
- Leave intended beneficiaries struggling financially,
- Disrespect and dishonor the wishes of the deceased,
- Erode trust in the legal system and estate planning process,
- Cause emotional trauma that can last for years, and
- Undermine the fabric of social responsibility and ethical conduct.

At Hackard Law, we've seen families torn apart by these disputes. Siblings who once were close become bitter enemies. Children feel betrayed by stepparents. Grandchildren are cut off from their inheritance. The emotional and moral toll can be just as devastating as the financial loss.

While many inheritance disputes stem from malicious intent, it's important to recognize that some arise from the natural evolution of family circumstances. As we'll explore in later chapters, even well-crafted estate plans may require adaptation over time. Trust modifications, when pursued ethically and with the consent of all parties, can be a legitimate way to honor a loved one's intentions while addressing unforeseen changes.

This underscores the importance of flexibility in estate planning and the value of open communication among beneficiaries. Our exploration will cover not just how to prevent and combat inheritance heists, but also how to navigate the complex waters of estate planning with integrity and foresight.

THE LEGAL LANDSCAPE

Combating inheritance heists requires a deep understanding of estate law, probate procedures, and litigation strategies. Our approach to these cases recognizes that while legal competence is essential, it must be paired with a broader understanding of moral responsibility and social justice. We strive to integrate ethical principles into our practice, considering not just individual client interests, but also the broader implications for family harmony and social good.

In California, where much of our practice is focused, we navigate a complex legal landscape that includes:

- The Probate Code, which governs the administration of estates,
- The Elder Abuse and Dependent Adult Civil Protection Act, which provides additional protections for vulnerable adults, and

- Case law that has shaped the interpretation of statutes and the handling of estate disputes.

Each case presents unique challenges, requiring a tailored approach. Sometimes, early intervention can prevent a heist before it occurs. In other cases, litigation becomes necessary to right a wrong that has already been committed.

Increasingly, we're finding that alternative dispute resolution methods, particularly mediation, can play a crucial role in resolving inheritance conflicts. As we'll explore in Chapter 6, mediation offers a way to navigate complex family dynamics, address emotional grievances, and find creative solutions that may not be possible through traditional litigation. This approach can often preserve relationships and honor the true intentions of the deceased in ways that a court battle cannot.

MY JOURNEY AND EXPERIENCE

In my previous books, *The Wolf at the Door: Undue Influence and Elder Financial Abuse* and *Alzheimer's, Widowed Stepmothers & Estate Crimes*, I've explored various aspects of estate litigation and elder law. Each of these works drew upon my personal experiences in both life and law to provide readers with crucial insights. This book, *Inheritance Heists*, builds upon that foundation to address a specific and increasingly prevalent issue in estate planning and probate law.

My journey in this field began nearly five decades ago, and over the years I've honed my skills and deepened my understanding of the complexities involved in estate disputes. As the founder of Hackard Law, I've built a team of dedicated professionals who share my commitment to protecting the rights of heirs and honoring the wishes of the deceased.

Our firm's focus on contingency fee estate, trust, and financial elder abuse litigation has allowed us to represent clients who might otherwise be unable to afford legal representation. This model, which we explore in depth in Chapter 7, aligns our interests with those of our clients, ensuring that we're fully invested in achieving the best possible outcome.

WHAT THIS BOOK OFFERS

The pages that follow will guide you through the murky waters of inheritance disputes, illuminating the tactics used by those who would subvert a testator's wishes for personal gain. We'll explore real-world cases, dissect common schemes, and provide practical advice for protecting your legacy or fighting back against unjust enrichment.

Specifically, this book will:

Identify common tactics: We'll explore the various methods used by perpetrators of inheritance heists, from emotional manipulation to document forgery. This includes an in-depth look at how dishonesty and deception play a role in these disputes, from both clients and opposing parties.

Provide preventive strategies: Learn how to protect yourself and your loved ones from becoming victims of these schemes. We'll also discuss strategies for promoting honesty and transparency in estate matters.

Explain legal remedies: Understand the legal options available if you suspect or have fallen victim to an inheritance heist. This includes navigating the complex ethical dilemmas that arise when dealing with dishonesty in legal proceedings.

Offer practical guidance: Get step-by-step advice on what to do if you find yourself embroiled in an inheritance dispute. We'll cover how to handle situations where you suspect deception, whether from your own client or the opposing party.

Explore digital asset challenges: We'll delve into the complexities of cryptocurrency and digital asset inheritance, using real-world cases to illustrate the unique challenges these modern assets present.

Master mediation techniques: We'll explore how mediation can be an effective tool in resolving inheritance disputes, preserving family relationships, and addressing the complex emotional landscape that often accompanies these conflicts. Chapter 6 delves deep into the art of mediation negotiation, providing strategies for overcoming impasses and crafting durable agreements.

Understand contingency fee arrangements: Discover how contingency fee models are revolutionizing access to justice in estate and trust litigation, particularly through the lens of Hackard Law's pioneering approach.

Share real-world examples: Through anonymized case studies, we'll illustrate how these situations unfold in real life and how they can be resolved. These examples will showcase the complexities of dealing with dishonesty in inheritance disputes.

Explore ethical considerations: We'll delve into the ethical challenges faced by legal professionals when confronted with client dishonesty or opposing party deception, providing insights into how to maintain integrity while zealously advocating for clients.

Analyze trust distribution disasters: We will explore the breakdown of trust distribution failures, analyzing how even thoughtfully designed estate plans can go awry. Through case studies and expert analysis, we'll examine the common pitfalls in trust creation and administration and provide strategies for avoiding these costly mistakes.

Identify and Prevent Caregiver Exploitation: We will examine the unique challenges presented by caregiver relationships, focusing on identifying signs of exploitation and establishing measures to safeguard vulnerable elders. We'll explore the mechanics of undue influence in caregiving relationships, discuss legal definitions of caregivers, and provide strategies for preventing and addressing caregiver exploitation.

Understand legal definitions: We'll explore important legal definitions, such as what constitutes a "caregiver" or "care custodian" under the law. As we'll see in Chapter 8, these definitions can be surprisingly complex and have significant implications in inheritance disputes.

Explore the emotional landscape: We'll examine the profound impact of grief and other emotions on inheritance disputes. Chapter 9 provides insights into how these emotions affect decision-making and offers strategies for legal professionals to navigate these sensitive waters.

Address cultural nuances: We'll examine how cultural backgrounds can influence approaches to inheritance and conflict resolution, providing guidance for navigating these complexities in mediation and legal proceedings.

Examine the presumption of fraud: We'll explore how the law views certain bequests with suspicion, particularly those made to caregivers, will drafters, and others in positions of trust. We will delve into the legal concept of presumption of fraud, its application in inheritance disputes, and strategies for both proving and defending against claims of undue influence.

Navigate stepparent inheritance conflicts: We'll look at into the unique challenges posed by stepparent scenarios in inheritance disputes, exploring common patterns, legal considerations, and strategies for preventing and resolving these conflicts.

Explore ethical integration: We'll examine how legal practitioners can integrate moral principles with professional expertise, serving both justice and the common good.

Address social responsibility: We'll discuss how preventing inheritance heists serves not just individual clients, but contributes to the broader social fabric and ethical foundation of our communities.

Throughout the book, we'll pay special attention to the unique challenges posed by caregiving relationships in the context of inheritance. As we'll explore in Chapter 8, caregivers can play a pivotal role in both protecting and, unfortunately, sometimes exploiting vulnerable elders. Understanding the dynamics of these relationships, the legal framework surrounding them, and the potential for abuse is crucial in our mission to stop inheritance heists.

A CALL TO ACTION

Always remember that knowledge is your strongest defense. By understanding both the legal and moral dimensions of inheritance heists, you can take proactive steps to protect your family's legacy or seek justice when wrongdoing occurs.

With nearly fifty years of legal experience, an AV Preeminent rating for more than thirty-five years, and recognition as a Super Lawyer, I bring a wealth of proficiency to this critical issue. But beyond professional accolades, I bring a deep commitment to ethical practice and the belief that legal expertise must serve both justice and human flourishing.

Inheritance heists are not just a legal problem; they're a moral one. They represent a betrayal of trust and a perversion of family bonds. By shining a light on these practices and providing tools to combat them, we can work towards a future where the final wishes of our loved ones are respected and honored, and where legal practice serves both justice and the common good.

Let's begin our exploration of this critical issue with the goal of ensuring that legacies are protected, families are preserved, and justice is served. Together, we can stop inheritance heists and safeguard the intentions of those who have entrusted us with their final wishes.

PART ONE

CHAPTER 1
WHEN GOOD INTENTIONS GO AWRY: TRUST DISTRIBUTION DISASTERS

Picture this: A once-close family gathered in a lavish living room, tension thick enough to cut with a knife. First-generation Italian siblings who once shared secrets and built a thriving family business together now glare at each other from opposite corners. Their elderly mother, once the beating heart of the family, sits quietly at the kitchen table, tears glistening in her eyes. This scene, heartbreaking as it is, has become all too common when family trusts crumble under the weight of greed, disharmony, mismanagement, or simple misunderstanding.

THE TICKING TIME BOMB OF TRUSTS

Trust distribution disasters aren't just the stuff of TV dramas or sensationalized headlines. They're real, painful problems that play out in homes, farms, businesses, law offices, and courtrooms across the country with alarming frequency. What's more unsettling is that they can affect any family, regardless of their wealth or background.

In fact, it's a far bigger issue than most people realize. According to a study by the Society of Trust and Estate Practitioners, a staggering 65% of trust disputes involve claims of trustees failing to fulfill their fiduciary duties. This isn't just a few isolated incidents; it's a widespread problem that's leaving a trail of broken families and depleted bank accounts in its wake.

Recent statistics paint a concerning picture of the state of estate planning in America:

- A 2021 Gallup poll found that only 46% of Americans have a will. This low rate of estate planning increases the chances of ambiguity and disputes.
- Even more alarmingly, a study by Caring.com revealed that 67% of Americans don't have an estate plan at all. This lack of planning can lead to more ambiguities when assets are distributed.
- The American Bar Association reports that will contests occur in 0.5% to 3% of estates. While this may seem low, it represents thousands of cases each year, many involving ambiguous language.
- A survey by BMO Wealth Management found that 40% of respondents reported family conflict after the death of a loved one. Ambiguous wills and trusts can exacerbate these conflicts.
- The National Association of Estate Planners & Councils reports that over 120 million Americans don't have up-to-date estate plans. Outdated plans can lead to ambiguities as circumstances change.
- Perhaps most shockingly, according to LexisNexis, approximately 55% of Americans die without a will or estate plan. This intestacy often leads to confusion and potential disputes among heirs.

These statistics highlight the prevalence of estate planning issues and the potential for ambiguities to arise, underscoring the importance of clear language in wills and trusts.

UNDERSTANDING TRUSTS: A BRIEF OVERVIEW

Trusts are powerful estate planning tools that have been helping families manage and protect their assets for generations. At its core, a trust is a legal arrangement where you, the trustor, transfer ownership of your assets to a trustee, who manages them for the benefit of your chosen beneficiaries. It's like appointing a guardian for your legacy, ensuring your wishes are carried out even after you're gone.

The primary purpose of most trusts is to avoid the often lengthy and expensive probate process. When assets are held in a trust, they can pass directly to your heirs without the need for court intervention, saving time, money, and preserving privacy. But trusts can do so much more. They can provide ongoing support for a child with special needs, minimize estate taxes, and even protect your assets from creditors.

Types of Trusts

There are various types of trusts, each designed to serve specific purposes:

1. Living trusts allow you to maintain control of your assets while you're alive, with a successor trustee taking over management upon your death or incapacity.
2. Irrevocable trusts can't be easily modified once established, offering strong asset protection and potential tax benefits.
3. Testamentary trusts, created through your will, only come into effect after you pass away.

One of the beauties of trusts is their flexibility. You can tailor them to fit your unique family situation and financial goals. However, it's crucial to understand that trusts are not one-size-fits-all solutions. They require careful consideration and often the guidance of experienced legal professionals to set up correctly.

SIBLING SHOWDOWNS: CASE STUDIES IN TRUST AND WILL DISTRIBUTIONS

The Gabriel Case: A Trust Distribution Disaster

One particularly striking case involves the Brown family - a name we've assigned to protect the real family's identity. This case stands out as a stark reminder of how quickly things can unravel when trust and communication collapse.

The Brown family seemed picture-perfect from the outside. Margaret, a widowed mother, had four adult children who appeared to maintain close relationships despite the geographical distance between them. Three of the siblings lived on the East Coast, while the youngest, Gabriel, had settled on the West Coast.

Margaret had always been fair-minded, and her estate plan reflected this. She had arranged for all her assets, including a substantial life insurance policy, to be divided equally among her four children. It seemed like a foolproof plan to ensure family harmony after her passing.

However, life had other plans. Margaret suffered a severe accident that left her in a rehabilitation facility for two months. During this time, it became clear that her mental faculties were declining rapidly. When she finally returned home, she required round-the-clock care. Sarah, Michael, and Emily, who lived nearby, noticed alarming changes in their mother's behavior. She often appeared confused, sometimes even delusional - imagining her long-deceased husband was still alive or that people were stealing her money.

It was during this vulnerable period that Gabriel, sensing an opportunity, made his move. Under the guise of a caring son, he flew from California to visit his mother in New Jersey. But his intentions were far from pure. In a shocking turn of events, Gabriel managed to convince his mentally fragile mother to sign a power of attorney, granting him full control over all her financial affairs.

With this newfound power, Gabriel wasted no time. He swiftly changed Margaret's bank accounts to his name and withdrew a staggering $400,000 as a down payment to purchase a new home on the West Coast. In a move that would further isolate Margaret from her other children, Gabriel relocated her to his new home in California - all without informing his siblings.

Months passed before Sarah, Michael, and Emily realized the full extent of Gabriel's deception. They were left in the dark about their mother's condition and whereabouts, frantically trying to piece together what had happened. Meanwhile, Gabriel was busy rewriting

Margaret's will, ensuring he would be the sole beneficiary of her estate and life insurance policy.

Gabriel's manipulation didn't stop there. He convinced Margaret that he was the only child who truly cared for her, poisoning her mind against her other children. Margaret, in her confused state, was unaware that Gabriel was actively working to keep her other children away.

The final blow came with Margaret's passing. Even in death, Gabriel maintained his secrecy, keeping the news from his siblings. It was only through a chance encounter with the funeral home that Sarah, Michael, and Emily learned of their mother's demise.

Devastated and betrayed, the three siblings turned to Hackard Law for help. We took on their case, pursuing legal action against Gabriel for undue influence and elder financial abuse. After a hard-fought battle, we managed to secure a settlement that returned a substantial portion of the estate to Sarah, Michael, and Emily.

The Brown case serves as a sobering reminder of how vulnerable elderly individuals can be to manipulation, especially from those they trust most. It underscores the critical importance of setting up robust safeguards in estate planning, maintaining open communication among family members, and staying vigilant about the welfare of aging parents.

While the legal system provided some recourse for the wronged siblings, no courtroom victory could fully heal the deep familial wounds inflicted by Gabriel's actions. The Brown family's story stands as a cautionary tale, urging us all to prioritize transparency, communication, and ethical behavior in matters of inheritance and family trust.

The Lawson Inheritance: A Tale of Influence and Family Conflict

In the annals of estate law, certain cases stand out not just for their legal complexities but for the deeply human stories they tell. The tale you're about to read is one such case. While the core elements and legal principles remain true to events that unfolded in a Southern California county, the names, specific details, and locations have been altered to protect the privacy and confidentiality of those involved. This is the story of the Lawson family - a narrative that serves as both a cautionary tale and a reflection of the challenges that can arise when family dynamics collide with matters of inheritance.

As the calendar turned to January 2024, a family drama unfolded in the sun-soaked streets of a coastal community. At the heart of this tale was Albert Lawson, a man of eighty years whose life had been a testament to hard work and family values. Albert's story, while unique in its details, echoes the experiences of many families grappling with end-of-life decisions and the distribution of assets. As we delve into the Lawson inheritance, remember that while names and places may be changed, the emotions, conflicts, and legal principles at play are all too real for many families facing similar circumstances.

Albert had always been a man of fairness, instilling in his three children, Thomas, Daniel, and Emma, the importance of equality. "Split it evenly," he would often say when speaking of his estate, a sentiment reflected in his meticulously crafted estate planning documents. But as time wore on, Albert's health began to falter and with it, the carefully laid plans for his inheritance.

A Daughter's Devotion or Deception?

The year 2023 saw Albert's strength waning, his once-firm resolve now as fragile as autumn leaves. It was then that Emma, his daughter, moved into his coastal home. On the surface, it seemed a gesture of filial piety - a daughter caring for her ailing father. But beneath this veneer of devotion, a more complex narrative was unfolding.

As Albert's world shrank to the confines of his home, Emma's influence grew. The ATM card, once rarely used, now saw a flurry of activity - over eighty transactions, each withdrawing a piece of Albert's life savings. By the time the final tally was made, more than $40,000 had vanished from the account. But this was merely the beginning. Another $35,000 disappeared from his bank accounts, leaving a trail of financial breadcrumbs that would later lead to heated courtroom debates.

. . .

The Pivotal Visit

In a move that would later be scrutinized under the harsh light of legal inquiry, Emma took her father to visit an estate planning lawyer. What transpired in that office would upend years of carefully balanced family dynamics. When the dust settled, a new trust emerged - one that left everything to Emma, named her as the sole trustee, and explicitly disinherited her brothers.

As Albert's health declined further, Emma became the gatekeeper to his world. Thomas and Daniel found themselves on the outside looking in, their attempts to speak with their father thwarted at every turn. The once-open doors of familial communication had slammed shut.

A Death and a Discovery

When Albert finally succumbed to his infirmities, the family's fractures deepened. Emma waited a week before informing her brothers of their father's passing. It was only later, when Thomas and Daniel received copies of the revised trust, that the full extent of their disinheritance became clear.

Shocked and hurt, the brothers turned to Hackard Law, determined to challenge what they saw as a grave injustice. Their lawsuit aimed to set aside the trust, citing undue influence and their father's lack of capacity during its creation.

Resolution and Reflection

In the end, the case never saw the inside of a courtroom. A settlement was reached, allowing Emma to keep a portion of the trust assets, while Thomas and Daniel split the remainder. It was a compromise that left no one fully satisfied, but it brought an end to a chapter of family strife.

The Lawson inheritance, once a symbol of unity and fairness, had become a cautionary tale of how easily family bonds can fray when faced with the lure of wealth. As the dust settled on this legal battle, the true cost - measured not in dollars, but in trust and relationships - remained incalculable.

Key Takeaways

Clear communication: The importance of open, honest communication within families about estate plans cannot be overstated. Regular family discussions about inheritance wishes can prevent misunderstandings and conflicts.

Professional oversight: When a family member becomes a caregiver, it's crucial to have professional oversight of financial matters to prevent potential abuse or misuse of funds.

Regular legal review: Estate plans should be reviewed regularly, especially in light of changing family dynamics or health conditions. This ensures that the documents always reflect the true wishes of the individual.

Capacity considerations: When making significant changes to estate plans, especially in cases involving elderly individuals, it's important to ensure and document the person's mental capacity to make such decisions.

Mediation as a tool: While this case was settled out of court, many similar disputes benefit from professional mediation, which can help preserve family relationships while resolving conflicts.

The cost of conflict: Legal battles over inheritances often cost more than just money. The damage to family relationships can be irreparable, underscoring the importance of prevention and early intervention in disputes.

By sharing stories like the Lawson family's, we hope to illuminate the complex interplay of emotions, ethics, and law that often characterize estate disputes. It serves as a reminder of the importance of careful planning, open communication, and professional guidance in navigating the sensitive waters of family inheritances.

THE ANATOMY OF A TRUST DISTRIBUTION DISASTER

Traditional probate practice often treats trust distributions as purely technical exercises, focusing on accounting entries and procedural requirements. But through the lens of a career plaintiff's attorney, I see these situations differently. Each failed distribution represents real harm to real people - harm that demands aggressive advocacy to remedy. This perspective transforms how we analyze and approach these cases.

The Gabriel and Lawson cases, while dramatic, are far from unique. Trust distribution disasters come in many forms, each with its own set of challenges and consequences. Let's examine some of the most common issues that can lead to such disasters.

Unclear or Ambiguous Trust Language

One of the most frequent causes of trust distribution disasters is unclear or ambiguous language within the trust document itself. Consider the case of the "Misinterpreted Millions," where a wealthy entrepreneur left his estate "to be divided equally among my children and their families." This seemingly straightforward instruction led to years of litigation as the beneficiaries argued over whether "families" included spouses, whether stepchildren were considered, and how to account for families of different sizes.

The legal implications of vague trust documents are far-reaching. Courts may be called upon to interpret the settlor's intentions, a process that can be time-consuming, expensive, and ultimately unsatisfying for all parties involved. In some cases, the court's interpretation may be at odds with what the settlor actually intended, leading to distributions that don't align with the original vision for the trust.

· · ·

Unequal Distributions

While unequal distributions are not inherently problematic - there may be valid reasons for a settlor to distribute assets unequally - they can often lead to family discord and legal challenges. The emotional toll on families can be severe, as beneficiaries who receive less may feel undervalued or unloved.

Take the case of "The Forgotten Sibling," where a successful businessman left 90% of his estate to his eldest son, who had worked alongside him in the family business, and only 5% each to his two daughters. The daughters, feeling slighted, challenged the trust on grounds of undue influence, leading to a bitter legal battle that lasted years and ultimately destroyed the family relationships.

Timing Issues

The timing of trust distributions can also lead to significant problems. Premature distributions might leave beneficiaries without resources later in life, while delayed distributions could cause hardship for those counting on the inheritance.

A real-life example is "The Bankrupt Beneficiary" case. Here, a trust was set up to distribute assets to the settlor's children when they reached the age of throty-five. However, one child, deeply in debt, filed for bankruptcy at thirty-four. The bankruptcy trustee attempted to claim the beneficiary's share of the trust, leading to complex legal proceedings and significantly reducing the value of the inheritance.

Trustee Mismanagement

Trustees wield significant power over trust assets and bear the responsibility of managing them in the beneficiaries' best interests. When trustees fail in this duty, whether through incompetence, negligence, or malfeasance, the consequences can be dire.

A cautionary tale is that of "The Reckless Investor Trustee." In this case, a family friend named as trustee invested the bulk of the trust assets in high-risk cryptocurrency ventures against the express wishes of the settlor. When the crypto market crashed, the trust lost over 80%

of its value, leaving the beneficiaries with a fraction of their intended inheritance.

THE RIPPLE EFFECT: CONSEQUENCES OF DISTRIBUTION DISASTERS

The fallout from trust distribution disasters extends far beyond the immediate financial implications. Legal battles can drain the estate's resources, with attorney fees and court costs sometimes consuming a significant portion of the trust's value. Family relationships, once warm and supportive, can be irreparably damaged by the strain of litigation and perceived betrayals.

For beneficiaries, the financial consequences can be severe. Those counting on their inheritance for retirement, education, or other life goals may find themselves facing an uncertain future. In extreme cases, beneficiaries might face financial ruin, particularly if they've made commitments based on their expected inheritance.

Moreover, the value of the estate itself can be eroded through prolonged legal battles, poor management during disputes, or the necessity of selling assets quickly to satisfy court judgments or settlements.

PREVENTION STRATEGIES: AVOIDING THE DISTRIBUTION DISASTER

While no strategy can guarantee the prevention of all trust disputes, there are several steps that settlors, trustees, and beneficiaries can take to minimize the risk of a distribution disaster:

Clear and specific trust language: Engage experienced estate planning attorneys to draft trust documents with precise, unambiguous language.

Regular trust reviews and updates: Review and update trust documents periodically, especially after major life events or changes in family dynamics.

Choosing the right trustee: Select trustees carefully, considering not just their financial acumen but also their interpersonal skills and understanding of family dynamics.

Open communication with beneficiaries: Foster open dialogue about the trust's purposes and provisions to manage expectations and reduce the likelihood of surprises.

Professional legal and financial advice: Seek ongoing professional guidance to navigate complex legal and financial landscapes.

WHEN DISASTER STRIKES: NAVIGATION AND DAMAGE CONTROL

Despite best efforts, trust distribution disasters can still occur. When they do, it's crucial to act quickly and strategically:

- **Seek legal counsel**: Engage an experienced trust and estates attorney to understand your rights and options.
- **Consider mediation**: Before resorting to litigation, explore mediation or other forms of alternative dispute resolution.
- **Document everything**: Keep detailed records of all communications and financial transactions related to the trust.
- **Protect the assets**: If you're a trustee, take steps to secure and protect the trust assets during the dispute.
- **Maintain perspective**: Remember that family relationships are often more valuable than material assets. Strive to resolve disputes in a way that preserves these relationships where possible.

CONCLUSION: THE IMPORTANCE OF PROPER PLANNING

The Lawson family's story, and the many others like it, underscore the critical importance of careful trust creation and management. While trusts can be powerful tools for wealth transfer and estate planning, they require diligence, clarity, and ongoing attention to function as intended.

In this chapter, we've explored how trust distribution disasters can occur even with the best intentions. By understanding the anatomy of these disasters, we're better equipped to prevent them and to address them when they do occur. Remember that clear communication, professional oversight, and regular legal reviews are key to preventing trust distribution disasters.

As we move forward, we'll explore more specific strategies for creating robust, dispute-resistant trusts, and dive deeper into the legal and emotional complexities of trust administration. In our next chapter, we'll examine the role of trustees in more detail, exploring both their powers and their responsibilities in ensuring the smooth operation of a trust.

Checklist for Trust Creators

- Clearly define the purpose of the trust
- Use specific, unambiguous language in trust documents
- Choose trustees carefully, considering both financial acumen and interpersonal skills
- Consider including a clause for alternative dispute resolution
- Review and update the trust regularly

Questions to Ask Your Estate Planning Attorney

- How can we make the language in my trust as clear and specific as possible?
- What are the potential tax implications of my trust distribution plan?
- How can I protect my trust from potential challenges or contests?
- What mechanisms can we put in place to ensure proper trustee oversight?

- How often should I review and update my trust?

Remember, while this chapter provides a general overview, trust and estate law can be complex and varies by jurisdiction. Always consult with a qualified attorney for advice tailored to your specific situation.

CHAPTER 2
ADAPTING THE BLUEPRINT: WHEN LIFE OUTPACES ESTATE PLANS

In the sun-kissed neighborhoods of California, where dreams are as abundant as the orange groves, the White family found themselves navigating the complex waters of inheritance. Their story is not one of villains or heroes, but of real people facing life's unpredictable nature and the challenges it brings to even the most carefully laid plans. As we have seen, inheritance disputes often involve complex challenges, from issues with trust distribution to cases of deliberate fraud. The White family's tale, however, illuminates a different facet of this complex issue: the need for flexibility and adaptation in estate planning.

NANCY'S LEGACY: A FOUNDATION BUILT ON LOVE

Nancy White, a woman of foresight and compassion, had crafted her estate plan with the best of intentions. Her revocable trust, amended several times over the years, was a testament to her desire to provide for her three children long after she was gone.

The trust's structure was both thoughtful and pragmatic:

- Separate trusts for each of her three children
- Each funded with interests from a rental house owned by the separate trust

- Mandatory income payments to each child
- No principal distributions
- Termination upon complete liquidation of the rental houses or a child's death
- Assets passing to surviving siblings' trusts or Nancy's surviving heirs upon a child's death
- The siblings' children or issue would not inherit their parents' interest at the parent's death

This structure, utilizing separate trusts for each child, is a common estate planning strategy, particularly effective in blended families or when children have different financial needs. It was a plan that, on paper, seemed to cover all bases. But as we all know, life has a way of throwing curveballs when we least expect them.

Nancy's approach reflects the careful planning we advocated for in Chapter 1, where we discussed the importance of clear and specific trust language. By creating separate trusts for each child, Nancy aimed to avoid the kind of ambiguity that often leads to trust distribution disasters. However, as we'll see, even the most meticulously crafted plans can require adjustment as circumstances change.

STEVEN'S DILEMMA: WHEN LIFE TAKES AN UNEXPECTED TURN

Enter Steven White, one of Nancy's children. Far from being a schemer or a "bad guy," Steven found himself facing circumstances his mother could never have foreseen. Life had presented Steven with a situation that required a delicate balance between honoring his mother's wishes and addressing his family's current needs.

Steven's petition to modify his trust wasn't born from greed or a desire to circumvent his mother's intentions. Instead, it was a thoughtful response to changed family circumstances - the kind of changes that occur in every family over time, yet are impossible to predict. Such petitions for trust modifications are not uncommon, especially when family situations evolve beyond the original trust's provisions.

This scenario highlights a crucial point we touched upon in the introduction: the growing complexity of modern families and the challenges this poses for estate planning. As family structures evolve and change over time, estate plans must be flexible enough to accommodate these shifts while still honoring the original intent of the settlor.

THE PROPOSED MODIFICATION: A BRIDGE BETWEEN PAST AND PRESENT

Steven's request was simple yet profound:

- Modify his trust to include a power of appointment
- Allow for the creation of a lifetime trust for his wife, Susan
- Enable income payments to Susan if Steven predeceased her
- Ensure the principal would still ultimately pass as originally specified in the child's trust

This modification wasn't about altering the core of Nancy's plan. The principal would still flow as Nancy had intended. Steven was simply seeking to provide for his wife in a way that aligned with the spirit of his mother's wishes while addressing realities Nancy couldn't have anticipated. The use of powers of appointment and provisions for spouses in trusts are common estate planning tools, reflecting the need for flexibility in long-term financial planning.

Steven's approach here stands in stark contrast to deceptive tactics. Instead of resorting to dishonesty or manipulation, Steven chose to address the issue openly and legally, seeking a modification that would benefit his family while still respecting his mother's overall intentions.

THE UNDERLYING THEME: THE FLUIDITY OF FAMILY NEEDS

As we delve deeper into the White family's story, a powerful theme emerges: the inherent fluidity of family needs and the importance of adaptability in estate planning. Nancy's original plan, while well-intentioned, couldn't account for every possible future scenario.

Steven's actions highlight a crucial truth - that sometimes, honoring a loved one's legacy means adapting their plans to unforeseen circumstances.

This concept of adaptability echoes the lessons we learned from the Janssen case. Just as mediation provided a flexible solution to the Janssen family's inheritance dispute, trust modifications can offer a way to address changing family dynamics without resorting to contentious litigation.

Steven's petition wasn't made in isolation. He pointed to his aunt Beatrice, who had made similar changes to her own trust. This familial precedent suggests a broader recognition within the family that estate plans sometimes need to evolve. Moreover, Steven's belief that Nancy herself would have made these changes if not for her Alzheimer's adds another layer of poignancy to the situation. It underscores the challenge many families face when dealing with estate plans created before a loved one's cognitive decline - a significant issue in estate planning that often necessitates careful consideration and sometimes legal intervention.

This aspect of the White family's story touches on a critical point: the increased longevity of our population and the higher risk of cognitive decline that comes with it. As people live longer, there's a greater chance that their estate plans may need to be adjusted to account for changes in their mental capacity or family circumstances.

Perhaps most telling is the united front presented by the family. The petition stated that all current and contingent beneficiaries consent to the modification. This unanimity suggests that Steven's proposed changes aligned with the family's collective understanding of fairness and Nancy's true intentions. Such consensus is often crucial in trust modification cases, as courts are more likely to approve changes when all beneficiaries are in agreement and the modification doesn't violate the trust's material purpose.

The White family's approach here stands in stark contrast to other contentious scenarios. The Whites managed to navigate their inheritance issues with open communication and mutual understanding. This underscores a key point we've made throughout this book: that many inheritance disputes can be avoided or resolved through honest dialogue and a willingness to consider the needs and perspectives of all family members.

THE ROLE OF LEGAL COUNSEL

It's important to note the crucial role that legal counsel likely played in this scenario. Navigating the complex world of trust modifications requires expert guidance. An experienced estate planning attorney would have been instrumental in helping Steven understand his options, draft the petition for modification, and navigate the legal process.

Attorneys have ethical responsibilities in inheritance disputes. In Steven's case, his lawyer would have had to carefully balance the duty to advocate for Steven's interests with the obligation to ensure that the proposed modifications truly aligned with Nancy's original intent and didn't unfairly disadvantage other beneficiaries.

LESSONS FROM THE WHITE FAMILY

The White family's story offers valuable insights for anyone involved in estate planning:

Flexibility is key. Even the most carefully crafted plans may need adjustment as family circumstances change. Estate planners should consider building in mechanisms for flexibility, such as powers of appointment or provisions for trust modifications.

Communication matters. Open dialogue among beneficiaries can lead to mutually agreeable solutions. The White family's united front in supporting the trust modification highlights the power of transparent communication in resolving potential conflicts.

Intent over rigidity. Sometimes, honoring the spirit of a trust means being open to reasonable modifications. Courts and beneficiaries alike should consider the settlor's overall intentions rather than adhering rigidly to the letter of the trust document.

Legal pathways exist. The Probate Code often provides avenues for sensible trust modifications that don't interfere with the trust's material purpose. Beneficiaries facing changed circumstances should explore these legal options rather than resorting to deception or litigation.

Anticipate change. While it's impossible to predict every future scenario, estate planners can design trusts with built-in flexibility to accommodate potential changes in family dynamics or beneficiary needs.

Consider cognitive decline. As our population ages, it's increasingly important to plan for the possibility of cognitive decline. This might involve setting up mechanisms for trust modifications or appointing trusted individuals to make decisions if the settlor becomes incapacitated.

Seek professional guidance. The complexities of trust modifications underscore the importance of working with experienced estate planning attorneys who can navigate the legal nuances and help ensure that any changes align with the settlor's intentions and comply with relevant laws.

CONCLUSION: A MODEL FOR ADAPTIVE ESTATE PLANNING

As we close this chapter on the White family's journey, we're reminded that inheritance isn't just about assets and documents. It's about families navigating change together, honoring the past while adapting to the present. In California, where innovation is a way of life, the White family shows us that even in matters of inheritance, there's room for thoughtful evolution.

Their story isn't one of "inheritance heists" but of responsible stewardship - a family working together to honor Nancy's legacy while addressing the realities of their lives today. It's a testament to the enduring bonds of family and the power of adaptability in the face of life's inevitable changes.

The White family's approach offers a model for how families can navigate the complex waters of inheritance with grace, honesty, and mutual respect. By embracing open communication, seeking legal guidance, and remaining flexible in the face of changing circumstances, they avoided the pitfalls of deception and litigation that we've seen in other cases throughout this book.

As we move forward, let this story serve as an inspiration and a guide. It reminds us that with careful planning, open dialogue, and a willingness to adapt, we can create estate plans that not only distribute assets fairly but also strengthen family bonds and honor the true legacy of our loved ones.

The White family's story illustrates that stopping inheritance heists isn't just about preventing malicious acts—it's also about creating flexible estate plans that can adapt to changing family circumstances. As we continue our exploration, remember that open communication and a willingness to consider modifications can help preserve family harmony and truly honor a loved one's legacy.

CHAPTER 3
NO WIN, NO FEE: HOW CONTINGENCY ARRANGEMENTS TRANSFORM ESTATE LITIGATION

In the complex world of estate and trust litigation, where family fortunes and legacies hang in the balance, access to quality legal representation can often be the deciding factor between justice served and inheritance lost. Hackard Law has pioneered a revolutionary approach that's changing the game in California: contingency fee estate and trust litigation.

As we've explored in previous chapters, from unraveling cryptocurrency estates to navigating complex family mediations, inheritance disputes require not just legal expertise, but also innovative thinking and a willingness to take calculated risks.

This chapter delves into how Hackard Law's contingency fee model is breaking down barriers, leveling the playing field, and setting new standards in the field of estate and trust litigation.

REVOLUTIONIZING ACCESS TO JUSTICE IN INHERITANCE DISPUTES

Probate is the court-supervised legal process of validating a deceased person's will (if they had one), paying their debts, and distributing their assets to heirs. In California, probate is generally required for estates worth more than $166,250, unless the deceased person's assets were held in a trust or had designated beneficiaries.

California probate lawyers are typically paid in one of two ways:

1. Statutory Fees: Under California Probate Code sections 10800 and 10810, both the attorney and the executor/administrator are entitled to statutory fees based on the gross value of the probate estate:

- 4% of the first $100,000
- 3% of the next $100,000
- 2% of the next $800,000
- 1% of the next $9 million
- 0.5% of the next $15 million
- A reasonable amount determined by the court for amounts above $25 million

2. Hourly Rates: For "extraordinary services" that go beyond routine probate matters (like tax disputes, property sales, or litigation), attorneys can petition the court for additional compensation based on their hourly rates.

The world of probate has long been one of the most conservative corners of legal practice. It can provide a predictability that is lacking in other parts of the law. Most probate attorneys focus on careful estate planning, trust administration, and hourly-rate litigation when disputes arise. It's a practice area that tends to attract lawyers who prefer consistency and established procedures over the uncertainties of contingency work. Established procedures

My journey into probate litigation was anything but traditional. As a career plaintiff's attorney, I brought a fundamentally different perspective - one shaped by decades of standing up for individuals against powerful interests. While most probate litigators are comfortable working within the system's established rhythms, my experience fighting for plaintiffs taught me to question whether those rhythms truly serve the interests of justice.

When I proposed taking estate and trust litigation cases on contingency, the response from traditional probate practitioners was predictable: absolute skepticism. "That's not how probate litigation works," they said. But their objections revealed more about the conservative culture of probate practice than any actual barriers to contingency arrangements.

Traditional probate litigators, accustomed to the security of hourly billing, saw no reason to rock the boat. But my background representing plaintiffs gave me a different view. I'd seen too many families with valid claims priced out of the justice system by hourly rates. The same skills that served me well in plaintiff's work - evaluating cases, managing risk, and fighting for the underdog - translated perfectly to estate litigation.

This willingness to challenge probate's conservative conventions wasn't just about fee arrangements. It was about recognizing that many vulnerable individuals - elderly parents, disinherited children, exploited beneficiaries - needed an advocate willing to take risks on their behalf. While traditional probate practice often focuses on maintaining order and following established procedures, our plaintiff-oriented approach focuses on righting wrongs and giving voice to those who have been silenced.

The contingency model we pioneered isn't just about expanding access to justice (though that's crucial). It's about bringing a more dynamic, advocacy-oriented approach to a practice area that too often favors the status quo over fairness. Our success has shown that probate litigation doesn't have to be bound by its conservative traditions - it can and should be a tool for championing the rights of those who can't stand up for themselves.

JUSTICE AND ADVOCACY FOR THE VULNERABLE

Before we dive into the legal intricacies, it's crucial to understand the moral weight that many cultures, particularly those influenced by Judeo-Christian ethics, place on justice and advocacy for the vulnerable. The Bible, a cornerstone of Western moral thought, has much to say about the importance of defending the rights of the disadvantaged:

> "Speak up for those who cannot speak for themselves, for the rights of

all who are destitute. Speak up and judge fairly; defend the rights of the poor and needy." (Proverbs 31:8-9)

This proverb encapsulates the essence of what contingency fee arrangements aim to achieve - providing a voice and access to justice for those who might otherwise be unable to afford it.

THE CONTINGENCY FEE MODEL: ALIGNING INTERESTS AND EXPANDING ACCESS

Traditionally, estate and trust litigation has been the domain of hourly billing, often putting quality legal representation out of reach for many deserving beneficiaries and heirs. Hackard Law's contingency fee model changes this paradigm:

- **Alignment of Interests**: We only get paid if we win, ensuring our goals are fully aligned with our clients'.
- **Access to Justice**: Clients can pursue valid claims without the burden of upfront legal fees.
- **Risk Sharing**: We shoulder the financial risk of litigation, demonstrating our confidence in the cases we take on.
- **Efficiency Incentive**: The model encourages us to resolve cases as efficiently as possible, benefiting both clients and the legal system.

The Consumer Attorneys of California (CAOC) emphasizes the importance of contingency fees in providing access to justice:

"A contingency fee is designed to expand access to the courts by making it easier for those without the financial means to pay for legal services. In a typical contingency fee agreement, the plaintiff is only responsible for paying their attorney if they win the case, with the payment coming as a percentage of the winnings."

THE BROADER IMPACT OF CONTINGENCY FEES ON CONSUMER PROTECTION

The significance of contingency fee arrangements extends far beyond estate and trust litigation. These fee structures play a crucial role in protecting consumers and holding wrongdoers accountable across various legal domains.

Leveling the Playing Field: Contingency fees enable individuals to take on powerful entities that might otherwise be untouchable. As noted by the CAOC:

> "Contingency fees help maintain equal footing in our courts between wealthy and powerful corporations and the average Californian who lacks the economic clout to afford high-priced corporate attorneys."

This leveling effect is particularly important in cases involving large corporations or institutions with substantial legal resources.

Deterring Misconduct: The availability of contingency fee arrangements serves as a deterrent to potential wrongdoers. Knowing that individuals have access to legal representation regardless of their financial means can discourage unethical behavior and encourage compliance with laws and regulations.

Promoting Efficiency and Merit-Based Cases: Contrary to some misconceptions, contingency fees actually promote efficiency and discourage frivolous lawsuits. The CAOC explains:

> "Contingent fees promote efficiency and discourage frivolous lawsuits. Since attorneys bear all the financial risk if there is no recovery or if the recovery does not cover their costs, they act as gatekeepers - not accepting frivolous or unjustified lawsuits."

. . .

This self-regulating aspect of contingency fees helps ensure that only meritorious cases are pursued, benefiting both the legal system and society at large.

HACKARD LAW'S UNIQUE POSITION IN THE CALIFORNIA LEGAL LANDSCAPE

As the leading estate and trust contingency fee law firm in California, Hackard Law brings unparalleled expertise and resources to each case:

Depth of Experience: Our team has successfully litigated hundreds of estate and trust cases on a contingency basis.
Statewide Reach: We have the capacity to handle cases throughout California, from San Diego to San Francisco.
Multidisciplinary Approach: Our attorneys combine deep experience in estate law, litigation, and financial forensics.
Track Record of Success: Our contingency model has resulted in tens of millions of dollars recovered for clients.

CASE STUDY: THE RODRIGUEZ FAMILY TRUST DISPUTE

To illustrate the power of Hackard Law's contingency fee approach, consider the case of the Rodriguez Family Trust.

Maria Rodriguez, a successful restaurateur, left behind a substantial estate upon her passing. Her son, Carlos, suspected that his sister Elena had exerted undue influence over their mother in her final years, resulting in a trust amendment that heavily favored Elena.

Carlos approached several law firms, but the potential costs of litigation deterred him from pursuing the case. When he came to Hackard Law, we saw the merit in his claim and took on the case on a contingency basis.

Our team conducted a thorough investigation, uncovering evidence of Elena's manipulation; employed forensic accountants to trace hidden assets; utilized advanced e-discovery techniques to uncover crucial digital evidence; and engaged in strategic negotiations, leveraging our trial-readiness.

The result? A settlement that not only restored Carlos's rightful inheritance but also exposed Elena's wrongdoing. Without our contingency fee model, this justice may never have been achieved.

WHY CONTINGENCY WORKS FOR ESTATE LITIGATION

Law firms must demonstrate several characteristics to make them uniquely positioned to offer contingency fee arrangements in estate and trust litigation:

- **Deep Case Selection Experience**: Deep experience to accurately assess case merit and potential value.
- **Financial Stability**: Resources to sustain long-term litigation without pressuring clients for settlements.
- **Reputation as Trial Lawyers**: Willingness to go to trial often leads to more favorable settlements.
- **Efficient Case Management**: Proprietary systems streamline the litigation process, maximizing value for clients.
- **Network of Experts**: Relationships with top forensic accountants, investigators, estate planning experts, and other specialists crucial to building strong cases.

OVERCOMING CHALLENGES: HOW HACKARD LAW NAVIGATES CONTINGENCY COMPLEXITIES

Contingency fee arrangements in estate and trust litigation present unique challenges, which Hackard Law has systematically addressed:

- **Valuation of Non-Liquid Assets**: We've developed sophisticated methods for assessing the value of complex estate assets, from closely-held businesses to intellectual property.

- **Managing Client Expectations**: Our clear communication protocols ensure clients understand the process and potential outcomes.
- **Balancing Risk and Reward**: Our case assessment matrix helps us make informed decisions about which cases to take on contingency.
- **Ethical Considerations**: We've established strict internal guidelines to ensure our contingency arrangements always prioritize client interests and comply with all ethical standards.

THE BROADER PERSPECTIVE: CONTINGENCY FEES AND ACCESS TO JUSTICE

The importance of contingency fees in providing access to justice cannot be overstated. As noted by the American Association for Justice:

> "The contingency fee system is the 'key to the courtroom' for thousands of Americans. It allows people who suffered an injury to bring a suit without having to have the money up front to pay their attorney."

This system is particularly crucial in cases where individuals have been wronged by powerful entities or in complex litigation that requires significant resources. Without contingency fees, many valid claims would never see the light of day, effectively denying justice to those who need it most.

THE ECONOMIC RATIONALE FOR CONTINGENCY FEES

From an economic perspective, contingency fees serve as an efficient mechanism for allocating risk and resources in the legal system. As explained by legal scholars:

> "Contingency fees allow for a more efficient allocation of risk between attorneys and clients. Attorneys, who are typically in a better position to assess and bear the risks of litigation, take on the financial burden in exchange for a potentially higher reward."

This risk-sharing arrangement not only makes legal services more accessible but also aligns the interests of attorneys and clients, promoting more effective representation.

ADDRESSING CRITICISMS AND MISCONCEPTIONS

Despite their clear benefits, contingency fees have faced criticism from some quarters. It's important to address these concerns:

Excessive Fees: Critics argue that contingency fees can result in attorneys receiving disproportionately large payments. However, as the CAOC points out:

> "Several recent studies have shown that, for the number of hours worked, median fees on a contingent basis are comparable to the median hourly fees of attorneys in similar cases."

Encouraging Frivolous Lawsuits: This common misconception is contradicted by the economic realities of contingency fee arrangements. As noted earlier, attorneys have a strong incentive to only take on meritorious cases.

Limiting Client Control: Some argue that contingency fees give attorneys too much control over cases. However, ethical guidelines and professional responsibilities ensure that client interests remain paramount.

THE FUTURE OF ESTATE LITIGATION: HACKARD LAW'S VISION

As we look to the future, Hackard Law is committed to further innovating in the field of contingency fee estate and trust litigation:

Expanding Access: We're exploring ways to make our services available to an even wider range of clients across California.
Technological Integration: Investing in AI and machine learning to enhance case analysis and prediction.
Educational Initiatives: Launching programs to educate the public and professionals about the benefits of contingency fee arrangements in estate disputes.
Policy Advocacy: Working with legislators to ensure laws support fair access to justice in inheritance matters.

CONCLUSION: CHAMPIONING JUSTICE IN INHERITANCE DISPUTES

We believe that access to quality legal representation shouldn't be limited by an individual's ability to pay upfront legal fees. Our contingency fee model for estate and trust litigation is more than just a business strategy – it's a commitment to justice and a recognition that every rightful heir or beneficiary deserves their day in court.

From unmasking deception to navigating complex family dynamics, the world of estate and trust litigation requires not just legal expertise, but also courage, innovation, and a deep commitment to justice. Hackard Law's contingency fee model embodies these qualities, ensuring that we stand shoulder-to-shoulder with our clients, fully invested in their success.

For professionals in the field of estate and trust litigation, our message is clear: the future of our practice lies in aligning our interests more closely with those of our clients. By embracing models like contingency fees, we can expand access to justice, deter wrongdoing, and ensure that the true intentions of testators are honored.

• • •

In the words of the Consumer Attorneys of California:

> "Without this system for financing litigation, our nation's bedrock, founding principles – that every individual matters and has the Seventh Amendment right to a fair trial – risk joining the rubble of civilizations lost to history."

At Hackard Law, we're committed to ensuring that these principles not only endure but thrive.

CHAPTER 4
THE EMOTIONAL LANDSCAPE OF INHERITANCE DISPUTES

In the realm of estate and trust litigation, the stakes are often not just financial but also deeply emotional. Family members navigating the complexities of inheritance disputes are frequently grappling with grief over lost relationships, the passing of loved ones, and the perceived injustices that can haunt them. This chapter aims to explore the intricate emotional landscape that accompanies these conflicts, particularly the grief experienced by family members, and the role that legal professionals can play in assisting them.

UNDERSTANDING THE STAGES OF GRIEF

Understanding the stages of grief is crucial for both clients and attorneys. The widely recognized model includes five stages:

1. **Denial**: Family members may initially struggle to accept the reality of the loss or the implications of the inheritance dispute.
2. **Anger**: Feelings of frustration and resentment towards siblings, fiduciaries, or the deceased can emerge, leading to heightened tensions.
3. **Bargaining**: Some may attempt to negotiate their way to a preferred outcome, often focusing on what might have been.

4. **Depression**: The weight of loss and conflict can lead to feelings of despair and hopelessness.
5. **Acceptance**: Ultimately, some may find a way to come to terms with the situation, allowing for potential healing and resolution.

Understanding these stages can help attorneys approach their clients with empathy and patience as they navigate their emotional responses.

THE IMPACT OF GRIEF ON DECISION-MAKING

Grief can impair decision-making abilities, causing clients to act irrationally or make impulsive choices influenced by emotion rather than logic. Legal professionals need to be aware of this and consider how grief affects:

Communication: Grieving clients may misinterpret intentions or feel threatened by opposing parties. Clear and compassionate communication is essential.
Timing: Decisions should not be rushed; grieving individuals might need more time to process information.
Support: Providing access to additional resources, such as grief counseling, can help clients manage their emotions more effectively during this turbulent time.

STRATEGIES FOR EFFECTIVE REPRESENTATION

Attorneys play a critical role in guiding clients through their grief while advocating for their interests. Here are key strategies:

Empathetic Listening: Allow clients to share their experiences and feelings without judgment.
Validation: Acknowledge their pain and frustrations, helping to affirm their emotions as normal in the context of loss.

Advocate for Mental Health Support: Encourage clients to seek help from mental health professionals who specialize in grief counseling.
Maintain Professional Boundaries: While it's important to be empathetic, attorneys must also set clear boundaries to ensure a constructive working relationship.

A MORAL PERSPECTIVE ON GRIEF

Much of our morality and values are informed by our religion. The Bible, the Torah, the Quran, and the Vedas all show examples of how we deal with loss and suffering.

Specifically, the Bible offers numerous examples of individuals grappling with loss and grief, providing insights that can inform our understanding and approach to these emotions in modern inheritance conflicts.

Old Testament Examples

Job's Grief: Perhaps the most profound example of grief in the Old Testament is found in the book of Job. After losing his children, wealth, and health, Job's response is a powerful illustration of raw grief: "Then Job arose and tore his robe and shaved his head and fell on the ground and worshiped. And he said, 'Naked I came from my mother's womb, and naked shall I return. The Lord gave, and the Lord has taken away; blessed be the name of the Lord.'" (Job 1:20-21) Job's grief is intense and physical, yet he maintains his faith. This demonstrates that even in the depths of sorrow, it's possible to hold onto one's core beliefs and values.

David's Lament: King David's grief over the death of his son Absalom is another poignant example: "The king was shaken. He went up to the room over the gateway and wept. As he went, he said: 'O my son Absalom! My son, my son Absalom! If only I had died instead of you —O Absalom, my son, my son!'" (2 Samuel 18:33) David's grief is unrestrained and emotional, showing that even powerful leaders are not immune to the pain of loss.

Abraham's Mourning: When Sarah died, Abraham mourned and wept for her: "And Sarah died at Kiriath-arba (that is, Hebron) in the land of Canaan, and Abraham went in to mourn for Sarah and to weep for her." (Genesis 23:2) This brief passage illustrates the importance of allowing time and space for mourning.

New Testament Examples

Jesus at Lazarus's Tomb: Even Jesus, who knew he would raise Lazarus from the dead, experienced grief: "When Jesus saw her weeping, and the Jews who had come with her also weeping, he was deeply moved in his spirit and greatly troubled. And he said, 'Where have you laid him?' They said to him, 'Lord, come and see.' Jesus wept." (John 11:33-35) This passage shows that grief is a natural and valid emotion, even when hope exists.

Paul's Comfort to the Thessalonians: Paul addresses grief in his letter to the Thessalonians: "But we do not want you to be uninformed, brothers, about those who are asleep, that you may not grieve as others do who have no hope." (1 Thessalonians 4:13) Paul acknowledges the reality of grief while offering hope as a source of comfort.

Religious Principles for Handling Grief

From these examples and other teachings, we can derive several principles for handling grief:

Acknowledge the Pain: Sacred texts don't shy away from depicting the raw emotions of grief. It's important to allow ourselves and others to express sorrow openly.
Seek Community: Many stories show people grieving together. In inheritance disputes, finding support from family, friends, or professional counselors can be crucial.

Maintain Hope: While experiencing grief, biblical figures often held onto hope. In the context of inheritance disputes, this might translate to maintaining faith.
Allow Time for Mourning: Most Holy boks recognize mourning as a process that takes time. In inheritance disputes, it's important to allow space for grieving losses – whether of relationships, expectations, or material inheritance.
Practice Forgiveness: Many religious teachings emphasize forgiveness, which can be a powerful tool in healing from the pain of inheritance disputes.

Applying Wisdom to Inheritance Disputes

In the context of inheritance disputes, these principles can guide both clients and attorneys:
Validate Emotions: Recognize that grief in inheritance disputes is valid and complex. It may involve mourning not just the deceased, but also lost relationships with living family members.
Encourage Support Systems: Advise clients to seek emotional support from appropriate sources, whether family, friends, or professional counselors.
Maintain Perspective: Help clients balance their immediate grief with long-term perspectives on family relationships and personal well-being.
Allow for Grieving: Understand that the legal process may need to accommodate periods of intense emotion and grief.
Promote Healing: Where possible, encourage paths to reconciliation and forgiveness, recognizing that emotional healing often transcends legal outcomes.

BALANCING EFFICIENCY AND EMPATHY: AN ATTORNEY'S PERSPECTIVE

As legal professionals dealing with inheritance disputes and elder abuse cases, we often find ourselves caught between two imperatives: the need for swift, decisive action to protect our clients' interests, and the importance of acknowledging and respecting the grief process our clients are experiencing. In my years of practice, I've come to recognize a personal challenge that I believe many attorneys in this field face. Our training and experience drive us to quickly identify what needs to be done and how to do it.

We're problem-solvers by nature and profession. However, this task-oriented approach, while necessary, can sometimes overshadow the emotional needs of our clients who are grappling with the loss of a loved one. It's a delicate balance. On one hand, time is often of the essence in these cases. Delay can mean the difference between preserving an estate and watching it disappear into the hands of unscrupulous caregivers or manipulative family members.

On the other hand, our clients are human beings experiencing one of life's most profound losses. Their grief is not just a sidebar to the legal issues at hand; it's an integral part of their experience and can significantly impact their decision-making process and overall well-being. I've learned, sometimes through missteps, that it's crucial to consciously make space for grief in our interactions with clients. This might mean:

- Taking a moment at the beginning of meetings to acknowledge the client's loss and emotional state.
- Being patient when clients need to process information more slowly or repeat questions.
- Offering resources for grief counseling or support groups alongside legal advice.
- Adjusting our communication style to be more empathetic and less clinical when discussing sensitive matters.
- Recognizing that what might seem like indecisiveness or irrationality could be a manifestation of grief.

It's an ongoing process of growth and self-awareness. There have been times when, in my drive to address the legal issues at hand, I've moved too quickly past the emotional aspects of a case. In those moments, I've learned the importance of stepping back, acknowledging my oversight, and offering a sincere apology.

These experiences have taught me that effective representation in inheritance and elder abuse cases isn't just about legal expertise and strategic action. It's also about emotional intelligence and the ability to navigate the complex interplay between legal necessities and human grief.

As we continue to fight against caregiver exploitation and other forms of inheritance heists, let's remember that our clients are not just cases to be solved, but people to be supported. By balancing our professional efficiency with genuine empathy, we can provide more holistic and effective representation, honoring both the legal and emotional needs of those we serve.

CONCLUSION

Recognizing and addressing the emotional landscape of inheritance disputes is crucial for legal professionals. By understanding the effects of grief and implementing compassionate strategies, attorneys can better support their clients during one of the most challenging times in their lives. This emotional insight not only fosters a better attorney-client relationship but also enables more effective advocacy throughout the legal process.

As we continue our mission to stop inheritance heists, understanding and addressing the role of grief is crucial. By recognizing the emotional complexities involved, we can provide more comprehensive and effective representation, potentially leading to resolutions that address both legal and emotional needs. This holistic approach, informed by timeless wisdom including biblical teachings, can help preserve family relationships and honor the true legacy of the deceased.

CHAPTER 5
THE TRUTH ABOUT LIES: WHEN DECEPTION TAINTS INHERITANCE

> "Keep your tongue from evil and your lips from speaking deceit." (Psalm 34:13)

THE DOUBLE-EDGED SWORD OF DISHONESTY

In the complex world of inheritance disputes, we often find that the ancient adage, "The first casualty when war comes is truth," attributed to U.S. Senator Hiram Johnson in 1917, holds disturbingly true. As families wage their own private wars over estates, trusts, and wills, truth often becomes the first victim, sacrificed on the altar of greed, revenge, or misguided self-preservation. As we've seen in previous chapters, these conflicts can tear families apart, but when lies enter the equation, the damage can be catastrophic and far-reaching. More importantly, how do we, as legal professionals, navigate the treacherous waters when deception comes not just from the opposing side, but from our own clients?

This chapter delves into the murky realm of dishonesty in inheritance cases, examining the motivations, consequences, and ethical dilemmas that arise when clients or opponents resort to lies. We'll explore the biblical perspectives on truthfulness, the legal implications of perjury, and the strategies for uncovering and dealing with deception from both sides of the courtroom.

THE WEIGHT OF TRUTH IN INHERITANCE

Before we dive into the legal intricacies, it's crucial to understand the moral weight that many cultures, particularly those influenced by Judeo-Christian ethics, place on truthfulness. The Bible, a cornerstone of Western moral thought, has much to say about the importance of honesty, especially in matters of justice and inheritance.

Consider these powerful verses:

> "You shall not bear false witness against your neighbor." (Exodus 20:16)

This commandment, one of the fundamental Ten Commandments, underscores the gravity of lying, especially in legal contexts.

> "Lying lips are an abomination to the Lord, but those who act faithfully are his delight." (Proverbs 12:22)

This proverb highlights the divine perspective on truthfulness, suggesting that dishonesty is not just a social wrong, but a spiritual offense.

> "Do not lie to one another, seeing that you have put off the old self with its practices." (Colossians 3:9)

This New Testament verse frames truthfulness as an essential part of moral and spiritual growth, suggesting that lying belongs to an old, unenlightened way of life.

These biblical injunctions against dishonesty provide a moral framework that many clients, regardless of their personal religious beliefs, may find compelling. They serve as a reminder of the ethical implications of lying, beyond just the legal consequences.

WHEN CLIENTS LIE: NAVIGATING THE ETHICAL MINEFIELD

As attorneys, we are bound by a code of ethics that requires us to represent our clients zealously while maintaining the integrity of the legal system. But what happens when we suspect or discover that our own client is lying?

The Motivations Behind Client Dishonesty
Fear of loss: The prospect of losing an expected inheritance can drive some to fabricate stories or conceal facts. This fear can be particularly acute when the inheritance represents financial security or the fulfillment of long-held expectations.
Revenge: Longstanding family grievances might motivate a client to lie to punish siblings or other relatives. In some cases, the inheritance dispute becomes a proxy for unresolved emotional conflicts.
Guilt: Paradoxically, a client might lie out of guilt, especially if they believe they're correcting a perceived injustice in the original estate plan. This can occur when a client feels they've been unfairly treated by the deceased or believes the estate plan doesn't reflect the deceased's true intentions.
Misunderstanding: Sometimes, what appears to be a lie might be a genuine misunderstanding of complex family history or legal documents. The intricacies of estate law and the emotional nature of family relationships can lead to sincere misconceptions.
Fear of rejection by legal counsel: An often overlooked motivation for client dishonesty is the fear that their case will be deemed too weak or problematic for an attorney to take on. Clients may embellish facts or conceal potentially damaging information in an attempt to make their case appear stronger or more straightforward than it actually is. This fear can be particularly strong if the client has already been turned down by other attorneys or if they believe their case is borderline. It's a misguided attempt to secure representation, born out of desperation or a lack of understanding of the legal process.
Shame or embarrassment: Clients may lie to cover up personal or family situations they find embarrassing. This could include issues like

estrangement from the deceased, past financial mismanagement, or personal struggles that they fear might weaken their claim.
Overconfidence in ability to control the narrative: Some clients, particularly those unfamiliar with legal proceedings, may believe they can control the entire narrative of their case through their initial statements. They might not realize the extent of the discovery process or the consequences of being caught in a lie.

Understanding these motivations is crucial for attorneys. It allows us to approach client interviews with empathy and skepticism in equal measure, probing gently but firmly to uncover the full truth. It also underscores the importance of creating an environment where clients feel safe to be honest, emphasizing that full disclosure, no matter how unflattering, is always preferable to a lie that could unravel their entire case.

THE ETHICAL DILEMMA FOR ATTORNEYS

When we suspect our client is lying, we face a serious ethical dilemma. On one hand, we have a duty to represent our client's interests. On the other, we have an obligation to the court and the legal system to not knowingly present false information. This dilemma becomes increasingly complex depending on when in the legal process we discover the dishonesty.

The American Bar Association's Model Rules of Professional Conduct provide some guidance. Rule 3.3 states that a lawyer shall not knowingly"make a false statement of fact or law to a tribunal or fail to correct a false statement of material fact or law previously made to the tribunal by the lawyer."

Rule 1.16 allows an attorney to withdraw from representation if "the client persists in a course of action involving the lawyer's services that the lawyer reasonably believes is criminal or fraudulent."

However, the practical application of these rules can vary depending on the stage of the legal process.

. . .

At the Beginning of Representation

If a lawyer discovers a client's lie during the initial consultation or early in the case, they have the most flexibility in addressing the issue.

The lawyer can confront the client, explain the importance of truthfulness, and potentially decline representation if the client insists on maintaining the lie.

Ethical Consideration: Balancing the duty to potential clients with the obligation to the legal system.

During Document Production

If a client provides falsified documents, the attorney must refuse to submit them to the court or opposing counsel. The lawyer should confront the client and demand honest documentation.

Ethical Consideration: Navigating client confidentiality while fulfilling the duty of candor to the tribunal.

During Depositions

If a client lies during a deposition, the attorney cannot allow the false testimony to stand. The lawyer should call for a break and confront the client privately, explaining the serious consequences of perjury. If the client refuses to correct the false testimony, the attorney may need to consider withdrawing from the case.

Ethical Consideration: Addressing false testimony without improperly disclosing client confidences.

At Settlement Conferences

If a lawyer learns of a client's lie during settlement negotiations, they cannot continue to rely on the false information in the negotiations. The attorney must persuade the client to correct the misinformation or withdraw from the negotiations.

Ethical Consideration: Balancing zealous advocacy with the duty of honesty in negotiations.

During Trial

This is perhaps the most challenging scenario. If a client lies on the stand, the attorney cannot allow the false testimony to stand uncorrected. The lawyer should request a recess and strongly urge the client to correct the testimony. If the client refuses, the attorney may be forced to inform the court that they can no longer vouch for their client's testimony.

Ethical Consideration: Upholding the duty of candor to the court while minimizing harm to the client's case.

After the Conclusion of Proceedings

If an attorney learns of a client's lie after the case has concluded, they may have an obligation to inform the court, especially if the lie materially affected the outcome. This could potentially lead to the reopening of the case or charges of perjury against the client.

Ethical Consideration: Balancing finality of judgments with the integrity of the legal system.

In all these scenarios, the overarching ethical principle is clear: an attorney cannot knowingly allow false information to be presented to the court. However, the specific actions required can vary based on the circumstances and timing of the discovery of the lie.

Navigating these ethical dilemmas requires a delicate balance of advocating for our clients, upholding the integrity of the legal system, and maintaining our own professional ethics. It often necessitates difficult conversations with clients and, in some cases, may lead to the termination of the attorney-client relationship.

STRATEGIES FOR DEALING WITH DISHONEST CLIENTS

Confront the issue directly: Have a frank conversation with your client about the importance of truthfulness and the consequences of lying.

Seek clarification: What appears to be a lie might be a misunderstanding. Ask probing questions to get to the truth.

Document everything: Keep detailed records of your conversations and advice to the client.

Consider withdrawal: If the client insists on lying, consider withdrawing from the case to maintain your ethical integrity.

WHEN THE OTHER SIDE LIES: UNMASKING DECEPTION

Dealing with dishonesty from the opposing party presents its own set of challenges. While we might feel more righteous indignation when facing an opponent's lies, we must be careful not to let this cloud our judgment or professional conduct.

Common Forms of Deception in Inheritance Disputes

Hidden assets: Concealing the true extent of the estate.

Fabricated debts: Creating false claims against the estate to reduce its value.

Altered documents: Tampering with wills or trust documents.

False accusations: Making unfounded claims of undue influence or lack of capacity.

Strategies for Uncovering and Countering Lies

Thorough discovery: Use depositions, interrogatories, and document requests to uncover inconsistencies.

Forensic analysis: Employ experts to examine documents for signs of alteration.

Witness interviews: Speak with family members, friends, and associates who might have relevant information.
Financial audits: Trace financial transactions to uncover hidden assets or fraudulent claims.

Legal Remedies for Opposing Party Dishonesty

Motions for sanctions: Request court penalties for discovery abuses or presenting false evidence.
Perjury charges: In severe cases, lying under oath can lead to criminal charges.
Amended pleadings: Update your legal filings to address newly uncovered deceptions.
Fee shifting: Ask the court to make the dishonest party pay your client's legal fees.

CASE STUDY: THE TANGLED WEB OF THE MARTINEZ ESTATE

To illustrate the complexities of dealing with dishonesty in inheritance disputes, let's examine the case of the Martinez estate. This case, based on a composite of real events with names and details changed to protect privacy, showcases how lies from both sides can complicate an already contentious situation.

Carlos Martinez, a successful restaurant owner, passed away and left a substantial estate to be divided among his three children: Elena, Miguel, and Sofia. The will specified an equal three-way split, but Elena, who had worked in the family business for years, believed she deserved a larger share.

As Elena's attorneys at Hackard Law, we initially took her claims at face value. She insisted that her father had promised her a controlling interest in the restaurant chain, even showing us a handwritten note that seemed to support her claim. However, as we prepared for litigation, inconsistencies in Elena's story began to emerge.

Meanwhile, Miguel and Sofia, represented by another firm, made counterclaims. They accused Elena of exerting undue influence over their father in his final years and misappropriating company funds. Their evidence seemed compelling, including bank statements showing large transfers to Elena's personal account.

As the case unfolded, it became clear that neither side was being entirely truthful:

- Elena's handwritten note turned out to be a forgery, created after her father's death.
- Miguel and Sofia's claims of financial misappropriation were exaggerated, based on legitimate business expenses they had misinterpreted.
- All three siblings had taken liberties with the truth regarding their levels of involvement in the family business and their relationships with their father.

This case presented significant ethical challenges for all attorneys involved. We had to confront Elena about her forged document, ultimately leading to our withdrawal from the case. The opposing counsel faced similar dilemmas with their clients' exaggerated claims.

The Martinez case ultimately settled through mediation, but not before the siblings' relationships were irreparably damaged and a significant portion of the estate was consumed by legal fees.

THE CONSEQUENCES OF DISHONESTY IN INHERITANCE DISPUTES

Legal Consequences
Case dismissal: Courts may throw out claims based on fraudulent evidence.
Sanctions: Monetary penalties, adverse inferences, or even default judgments can result from dishonesty.
Criminal charges: Perjury and fraud can lead to criminal prosecution.

Financial Consequences
Increased legal costs: Lies often extend litigation, dramatically increasing expenses.
Loss of inheritance: Dishonesty can result in a reduced share or total disinheritance.
Damages: Courts may award damages against parties who have lied or presented false claims.

Personal and Family Consequences
Broken relationships: Trust, once shattered by lies, is hard to rebuild.
Reputation damage: Dishonesty in legal proceedings can have lasting impacts on personal and professional reputations.
Emotional toll: The stress of maintaining lies and facing their consequences can be severe.

PROMOTING HONESTY: STRATEGIES ATTORNEYS USE

As legal professionals, we have a responsibility not just to navigate dishonesty, but to actively promote truthfulness in inheritance disputes.

Here are some strategies:
Set clear expectations: From the first client meeting, stress the importance of honesty and the consequences of lying.
Educate clients: Explain the legal process, including discovery and cross-examination, so clients understand how lies can be exposed.
Encourage communication: Promote open dialogue among family members when possible, which can prevent misunderstandings and reduce the temptation to lie.
Utilize alternative dispute resolution: Mediation and collaborative law approaches can create an environment more conducive to honesty.
Lead by example: Maintain the highest standards of honesty and integrity in your own practice.

In our ongoing mission to stop inheritance heists, understanding and addressing dishonesty is crucial. Whether from clients or opposing parties, lies can derail inheritance proceedings and destroy family relationships. By promoting a culture of honesty and having strategies to deal with deception, we can better protect the integrity of the inheritance process and the families involved.

CONCLUSION: THE TRIUMPH OF TRUTH

"The truth will set you free." (John 8:32)

In the complex world of inheritance disputes, where emotions run high and the stakes can be enormous, the temptation to bend the truth can be strong. However, as we've seen, the consequences of dishonesty – legal, financial, and personal – far outweigh any short-term gains.

As legal professionals, we must remain vigilant, not only in uncovering lies but in actively promoting a culture of honesty. By doing so, we not only serve our clients better but also uphold the integrity of the legal system and help preserve the familial bonds that are all too often casualties of inheritance disputes.

In the words of Proverbs 12:19, "Truthful lips endure forever, but a lying tongue lasts only a moment." In the realm of inheritance law, this ancient wisdom holds true. The momentary advantage gained by a lie pales in comparison to the lasting benefits of honesty, integrity, and justice.

CHAPTER 6
THE PRESUMPTION OF FRAUD: WHEN THE LAW SUSPECTS FOUL PLAY

In the complex world of inheritance disputes, not all gifts are created equal. The law casts a suspicious eye on certain bequests, especially those made to caregivers, drafters of wills or trusts, and others in positions of trust or influence. This presumption of fraud or undue influence serves as a powerful tool for would-be heirs looking to challenge a questionable inheritance.

WIELDING THE SWORD

The presumption of fraud is often treated by traditional probate practitioners as a technical doctrine to be carefully navigated. But through the lens of a career plaintiff's advocate, I see it as something far more powerful - a sword to be wielded aggressively in the fight against inheritance theft. This shift in perspective transforms how we approach cases where the presumption applies.

THE LEGAL LANDSCAPE

The California Probate Code, like many state laws, outlines specific situations where a donative transfer (a gift made through a will, trust, or other instrument) is presumed to be the product of fraud or undue influence. This legal presumption doesn't mean fraud definitely occurred, but it shifts the burden of proof to the recipient of the gift to show that everything was legitimate.

REAL-WORLD EXAMPLES

To illustrate how the presumption of fraud plays out in practice, let's examine some real-life scenarios:

The Caregiver's Windfall

Emma, an eighty-five-year-old widow with early-stage dementia, hires Maria as a live-in caregiver. Six months later, Emma changes her will to leave her entire $2 million estate to Maria instead of her children. When Emma dies a year later, her children challenge the will. The presumption of fraud applies, and unless Maria can produce clear and convincing evidence that she didn't unduly influence Emma, she'll lose the inheritance and may have to pay the children's legal fees.

The Lawyer's Mistake

Attorney John drafts a new will for his long-time client, Bob. As a gesture of appreciation, Bob insists on including a $50,000 bequest to John. Even if John can prove Bob was of sound mind and insisted on the gift, the presumption against drafting attorneys is conclusive. John will lose the bequest if challenged.

The Helpful Nephew

Linda, seventy, has her nephew Mark move in to help care for her after a stroke. Two years later, she leaves him her house in her will. Because Mark had a pre-existing family relationship and didn't charge for his care, the presumption of fraud doesn't apply. Linda's other relatives would have to prove undue influence without the benefit of the legal presumption.

Daughters Accused of Isolating Father

After a three-week trial, a jury ruled that the daughters of an elderly man with diminished mental capacity isolated him from their brother and used their influence to disinherit their sibling. The jury verdict allowed the brother to claim one-third of a trust and bank accounts worth about $3 million.

PROVING UNDUE INFLUENCE

Even with the presumption, proving undue influence can be challenging. Courts consider factors such as:

- The vulnerability of the victim due to illness, age, cognitive impairment, isolation, or dependency
- The authority and opportunity the influencer had over the victim
- The tactics used to influence the victim, like manipulation, coercion, or isolation
- Whether the resulting estate plan seems inequitable or illogical

It's important to note that just because someone develops a close relationship with the deceased or convinces them to change their will does not automatically constitute undue influence. There must be evidence that the influencer improperly pressured or deceived the victim.

PROTECTING AGAINST UNDUE INFLUENCE

For those making estate plans, getting a Certificate of Independent Review from an attorney can help insulate gifts from later challenges. Potential heirs suspecting undue influence should look for red flags like a vulnerable testator, a major change to long-standing estate plans, or a new influencer isolating the deceased. Working with an experienced probate litigator is crucial in these cases.

THE EMOTIONAL TOLL

As we have explored, inheritance disputes carry a heavy emotional burden. The presumption of fraud cases are no exception. Family members challenging a will or trust may be grappling not only with the loss of a loved one but also with feelings of betrayal, anger, and grief over perceived manipulation of the deceased.

For the accused, the emotional stakes are equally high. A caregiver who formed a genuine bond with the deceased may find themselves painted as a predator, their motives questioned and their reputation at stake. The presumption of fraud, while a necessary legal tool, can add layers of stress and hurt to an already painful situation.

BALANCING LEGAL STRATEGY AND EMOTIONAL SUPPORT

As legal professionals, we must be mindful of the emotional landscape when handling presumption of fraud cases. This requires balancing aggressive advocacy with empathy and understanding. Some strategies to consider:

- **Clear Communication**: Explain the legal concept of presumption of fraud clearly, helping clients understand what to expect from the process.
- **Emotional Preparation**: Prepare clients for the emotional toll of having their motives questioned or questioning a family member's actions.
- **Support Resources**: Provide referrals to therapists or support groups specializing in inheritance disputes and grief counseling.
- **Mediation Opportunities**: Where appropriate, consider mediation as a less adversarial approach that may preserve relationships.

CONCLUSION

The presumption of fraud serves as a critical safeguard in the realm of inheritance law, shining a spotlight on potentially questionable bequests and helping to level the playing field for heirs facing suspected manipulation. As we continue our mission to stop inheritance heists, understanding how and when this presumption applies is crucial.

However, we must also remain mindful of the human element in these cases. Behind every legal argument lies a story of family dynamics, personal relationships, and often, genuine care and affection. By approaching these cases with a balance of legal acumen and emotional intelligence, we can work towards resolutions that not only satisfy the letter of the law but also honor the spirit of the deceased's wishes and preserve family bonds where possible.

In the high-stakes game of inheritance disputes, the presumption of fraud is a powerful piece on the board. Wielded with skill and compassion, it can be a force for justice, helping to ensure that the true intentions of the deceased are honored and that vulnerability is not exploited for personal gain.

CHAPTER 7
MASTERING MEDIATION NEGOTIATION: THE ART OF RESOLVING INHERITANCE DISPUTES

In the complex world of inheritance disputes, where family ties are strained and emotions run high, mediation often emerges as a beacon of hope. It offers a path to resolution that can preserve relationships and avoid the costly, time-consuming battles of litigation. This chapter delves into the art and science of mediation negotiation, exploring how parties can navigate this process to reach a settlement that honors the legacy of their loved ones while addressing the needs and concerns of all involved.

A MORAL PERSPECTIVE ON MEDIATION

As we've seen in previous chapters, incorporating biblical wisdom can provide valuable insights into complex family dynamics, especially when it is paramount that we try to preserve relationships.

In the context of mediation, several biblical principles are particularly relevant:

> "If your brother sins against you, go and tell him his fault, between you and him alone. If he listens to you, you have gained your brother." (Matthew 18:15)

This verse emphasizes the importance of direct communication and private resolution of conflicts, which aligns closely with the principles of mediation.

> "Blessed are the peacemakers, for they shall be called sons of God." (Matthew 5:9)

This beatitude underscores the spiritual value placed on those who work to resolve conflicts, a role that mediators embody in inheritance disputes.

> "Let every person be quick to hear, slow to speak, slow to anger." (James 1:19)

This advice encapsulates key skills for both mediators and parties in mediation: active listening, thoughtful communication, and emotional regulation.

THE MEDIATION LANDSCAPE: A DIFFERENT KIND OF BATTLEFIELD

As we've seen in previous chapters, inheritance disputes can quickly spiral into all-out legal warfare. The Martinez siblings' case demonstrated how lies and deception can escalate conflicts, while the O'Sullivan family's cryptocurrency saga highlighted the complexities that modern assets bring to these disputes. Mediation offers an alternative - a structured yet flexible process where parties can work towards a mutually acceptable solution.

In mediation, the battleground shifts from the courtroom to the conference room. Instead of attorneys arguing before a judge, we find family members, their legal representatives, and a neutral mediator engaged in a delicate dance of negotiation. The weapons here are not legal precedents and witness testimonies, but rather open communication, creative problem-solving, and a willingness to find common ground.

THE MEDIATOR'S ROLE: NAVIGATING TROUBLED WATERS

At the heart of any successful mediation is a skilled mediator. This neutral third party plays a crucial role in guiding the process, much like a seasoned captain navigating a ship through stormy seas.

The mediator's toolkit includes:

- Facilitation: Creating an environment conducive to open dialogue and productive negotiation.
- Reality Testing: Helping parties evaluate the strengths and weaknesses of their positions.
- Reframing: Assisting parties in seeing issues from different perspectives.
- Generating Options: Encouraging creative solutions that may not be available through litigation.

A skilled mediator must be adept at handling complex family dynamics and untangling the web of emotions that often cloud inheritance disputes.

PREPARATION: THE FOUNDATION OF SUCCESSFUL NEGOTIATION

Thorough preparation is crucial for successful negotiation, especially in mediation where the stakes are high and the opportunities for direct negotiation may be limited. Key preparation strategies include:

Assessing Your BATNA: Understanding your "Best Alternative to a Negotiated Agreement" is crucial. In inheritance disputes, this often means evaluating the likely outcome of litigation.
Calculating Your Reservation Value: Knowing your "walk-away" point helps you avoid accepting an unfavorable settlement out of desperation.
Evaluating the ZOPA: The Zone of Possible Agreement represents the

range within which a deal is possible. Understanding this helps in crafting realistic proposals.
Developing a Scoring System: Assigning relative values to different issues helps prioritize and make trade-offs during negotiation.

THE ART OF COMMUNICATION: SPEAKING AND LISTENING WITH PURPOSE

Effective communication is the lifeblood of successful mediation negotiation. As we saw in the White family's story, open and honest dialogue can lead to mutually agreeable solutions, even when dealing with complex trust modifications. Key communication strategies include:

Active Listening: Truly hearing and understanding the other party's concerns and motivations.
Asking Probing Questions: Questions like "How does this deal fit into your overall family strategy?" can reveal valuable information.
Labeling Concessions: Making it clear when you're making a concession can encourage reciprocity from the other party.
Managing Emotions: In highly charged family disputes, keeping emotions in check is crucial for productive negotiations.

NEGOTIATION TACTICS: THE CHESS GAME OF MEDIATION

Mediation negotiation is a strategic endeavor, not unlike a game of chess. Each move should be carefully considered, with an eye towards the ultimate goal of reaching a mutually acceptable agreement. Some key tactics include:

Anchoring: Making the first offer can set the stage for the negotiation, but it must be done carefully to avoid alienating the other party.
Disaggregating Gains and Aggregating Losses: People prefer to find money in installments but lose it in one lump sum. This principle can be applied to structuring settlement offers.

Using the "Door in the Face" Technique: Starting with a more extreme request can make a subsequent, more reasonable request seem more attractive. That said, I always advise that it not be so extreme that the other side will leave the mediation.

Making Multiple Offers Simultaneously: Presenting several options can help identify the other party's priorities and increase the chances of finding common ground.

NAVIGATING GRIEF IN MEDIATION

Inheritance disputes often occur in the wake of a loved one's passing, adding an extra layer of complexity to the mediation process. Grief can profoundly affect negotiation dynamics, and it's crucial for mediators and attorneys to understand and address these impacts.

How Grief Affects Negotiation Dynamics

Emotional Volatility: Grieving parties may experience sudden mood swings or outbursts, making negotiations unpredictable.

Difficulty in Decision-Making: Grief can cloud judgment and make it challenging for parties to evaluate offers objectively.

Attachment to Symbolic Items: Seemingly insignificant objects may hold deep emotional value for grieving parties, complicating asset division.

Desire for Closure: Some grieving parties may rush to settle to achieve a sense of finality, potentially agreeing to unfavorable terms.

Techniques for Mediators to Address Grief-Driven Behaviors:

Acknowledge the Loss: Begin the mediation by recognizing the shared loss and allowing parties to express their grief.

Create a Supportive Environment: Ensure the mediation space feels safe and comfortable for emotional expression.

Use Caucuses Effectively: Private sessions can provide a space for parties to process emotions without the pressure of the other side's presence.

Employ Reflective Listening: Demonstrate understanding and empathy by reflecting back the emotions you observe.

Allow for Breaks: Be prepared to pause the mediation if emotions become overwhelming.

Reframe the Process: Help parties see the mediation as a way to honor the deceased's legacy rather than a battle over assets.

Strategies for Attorneys to Support Grieving Clients During Mediation:

Pre-Mediation Counseling: Prepare clients for the emotional challenges they may face during mediation.

Encourage Professional Support: Suggest grief counseling or therapy to help clients process their emotions outside of the legal process.

Focus on Interests, Not Positions: Help clients identify their underlying interests, which may be obscured by grief-driven positions.

Use Empathy and Patience: Understand that your client's grief may manifest in unexpected ways and be patient with their process.

Advocate for Breaks: Be prepared to request pauses in the mediation if you sense your client is becoming overwhelmed.

Help Maintain Perspective: Gently remind clients of their long-term goals when grief threatens to derail productive negotiations.

By integrating these strategies for navigating grief into the mediation process, mediators and attorneys can create a more supportive environment for resolving inheritance disputes. This approach not only leads to more sustainable agreements but also helps families begin the healing process in the wake of their loss.

OVERCOMING IMPASSE: STRATEGIES FOR BREAKING DEADLOCKS

Even in the most promising mediations, impasses can occur. The key is to view these not as roadblocks, but as opportunities for creative problem-solving. Strategies for overcoming impasse include:

Changing the Game: Introducing new issues or reframing existing ones can shift the dynamics of the negotiation.

Exploring Underlying Interests: Often, an impasse occurs because parties are focused on positions rather than interests. Digging deeper can reveal new avenues for agreement.

Using Contingent Agreements: When parties disagree about future events, contingent agreements can bridge the gap.
Taking a Break: Sometimes, a pause in negotiations can allow emotions to cool and new perspectives to emerge.
Changing the Physical Environment: Moving to a different room or taking a walk can shift perspectives and break through mental blocks.
Hypothetical Future Scenarios: Asking parties to imagine how they'd feel about the current impasse in five or ten years can often break through short-term thinking.
Blind Bidding: In cases where parties are stuck on numerical values, blind bidding can help. Each party submits their "final offer" privately to the mediator. If the offers overlap or are within a certain range, it forms the basis for a resolution.
Role Reversal: Having parties argue each other's positions can lead to increased empathy and understanding, often revealing new paths to agreement.

THE ETHICS OF MEDIATION NEGOTIATION: BALANCING ADVOCACY AND INTEGRITY

Ethical considerations play a crucial role in mediation negotiation. While zealously advocating for your client's interests, it's essential to maintain integrity and respect for the mediation process.

Key ethical considerations include:
Honesty in Information Sharing: While you're not obligated to reveal all information, actively deceiving the other party or the mediator is unethical and counterproductive.
Respecting Confidentiality: The confidentiality of mediation proceedings must be maintained to preserve the integrity of the process.
Balancing Power Dynamics: In family disputes, there may be power imbalances that need to be addressed to ensure a fair negotiation.
Avoiding Coercion: While it's acceptable to highlight the potential downsides of failing to reach an agreement, outright threats or coercion are unethical.

CRAFTING THE AGREEMENT: FROM NEGOTIATION TO IMPLEMENTATION

The ultimate goal of mediation negotiation is to reach a settlement agreement. This document translates the negotiated terms into a binding contract that will guide the parties' actions moving forward.

Key considerations in crafting the agreement include:
Clarity and Specificity: The agreement should be clear and specific to avoid future disputes over interpretation.
Comprehensiveness: All agreed-upon terms should be included, leaving no room for ambiguity.
Enforceability: The agreement should be structured in a way that makes it legally enforceable.
Implementation Plan: Including a clear plan for how the agreement will be carried out can prevent future conflicts.
Review Mechanisms: Building in periodic review sessions can help address unforeseen issues and maintain family communication.

CASE STUDY: THE JOHNSON FAMILY TRUST MEDIATION

To illustrate these principles in action, let's consider the case of the Johnson Family Trust mediation. This case, while fictional, draws on elements from various real-world scenarios we've encountered, demonstrating how effective mediation can resolve complex disputes even within a single day.

The Johnson family found themselves in a bitter dispute over their parents' trust. The three siblings - Sarah, Michael, and Emily - each had different interpretations of their parents' intentions and felt entitled to a larger share of the estate. With tensions high and communication breaking down, they agreed to a one-day mediation session as a last resort before litigation.

The mediator, Hon. Ed Greene (Ret.), began the morning with brief individual caucuses to understand each sibling's position:

Sarah, visibly stressed, insisted, "I gave up my career to care for

Mom and Dad. I deserve more!" Judge Greene used active listening, acknowledging Sarah's sacrifices while gently probing about her underlying needs.

In Michael's session, his fear became apparent when he confided, "My medical bills are piling up. I don't know how I'll manage if I don't get a larger share." Judge Greene reframed this concern, asking, "So, it's not about getting more than your siblings, but about ensuring your future healthcare needs are met?"

Emily, the youngest, was adamant about equal division. "It's what Mom and Dad would have wanted," she stated firmly. Judge Greene used reality testing here, asking, "If your parents knew about your siblings' current situations, do you think they might have considered a different approach?"

After these initial caucuses, Judge Greene brought the siblings together. Recognizing the emotional undercurrents, he began with a storytelling exercise, having each sibling share their fondest memories of their parents. This shifted the focus from the money to the family legacy they all shared, creating a more collaborative atmosphere.

As discussions progressed, Judge Greene employed the "expanding the pie" technique, asking, "Beyond money, what else in this estate has value to each of you?" This led to a breakthrough when Sarah mentioned their mother's art collection, Michael expressed interest in their father's rare book collection, and Emily showed attachment to the family vacation home.

Throughout the day, Judge Greene skillfully managed the siblings' emotions, calling for short breaks when tensions rose and using reframing techniques to keep the conversation productive. As the afternoon wore on, creative problem-solving was in full swing. Judge Greene used hypothetical scenarios to help the siblings see beyond their immediate concerns, asking questions like, "How would you want your own children to handle a similar situation in the future?"

By early evening, with Judge Greene's guidance, the siblings and their lawyers had crafted a comprehensive agreement that addressed each of their core concerns while preserving the spirit of their parents' legacy. The final agreement included:

- Equal division of monetary assets.
- A separate fund to reimburse Sarah for her caregiving expenses.
- A plan for managing shared assets like the vacation home, with scheduled time for each sibling's use.

The mediation, which began with hostility in the morning, ended with the siblings having certainty as to their inheritance and relief that their dispute would be resolved without years of expensive and emotionally exhausting litigation. Judge Greene's skilled facilitation had not only resolved the immediate financial dispute but had also laid the groundwork for healing long-standing family rifts.

CULTURAL CONSIDERATIONS IN INHERITANCE MEDIATION

Culture plays a significant role in how families approach inheritance and conflict resolution. Mediators must be culturally competent to navigate these complexities effectively, especially when working with diverse client backgrounds. Key cultural considerations include:

European-American Traditions
Individualism vs. Family Legacy: Many Americans with European ancestry value individual rights and equal distribution among heirs. However, some families may prioritize preserving family businesses or properties across generations.
Nuclear Family Focus: There's often a stronger emphasis on immediate family (spouse and children) in inheritance matters, compared to extended family.

Filipino Cultural Influences
Filial Piety: There's a strong emphasis on caring for elders, which can complicate inheritance disputes when some siblings have provided more care than others.
Extended Family Involvement: Decisions often involve extended

family members, not just immediate heirs. This can be complicated by extended family members living outside of the United States.

Conflict Avoidance: Direct confrontation may be seen as disrespectful, requiring mediators to use indirect communication strategies.

Hispanic Cultural Considerations

Familismo: The concept of prioritizing family needs over individual desires can influence inheritance expectations.

Gender Roles: Traditional gender expectations may impact how inheritance is viewed, particularly in first-generation families.

Religious Influences: Catholic traditions may play a role in how inheritance and family obligations are perceived.

African American Perspectives

Historical Context: The legacy of systemic inequalities may influence views on wealth preservation and distribution.

Oral Traditions: Verbal agreements or promises may hold significant weight, even if not legally documented.

Community Involvement: Extended family and community elders may play important roles in dispute resolution.

Cross-Cultural Factors

Generational Differences: First and second-generation Americans may have different views on inheritance compared to their parents or grandparents.

Language Barriers: Ensure clear communication, possibly involving interpreters for older family members.

Legal System Trust: Some immigrant communities may have varying levels of trust in the legal system, impacting their approach to formal mediation.

Mediation Strategies

- Use cultural brokers or co-mediators when appropriate to bridge cultural gaps.

- Be aware of non-verbal communication cues that may vary across cultures.
- Recognize that the concept of "fairness" in inheritance may differ based on cultural background.
- Allow for flexible timelines, as some cultures may require more time for family consultations.
- Be prepared to explain the U.S. legal framework around inheritance, as it may differ from cultural expectations.

By understanding and respecting these diverse cultural perspectives, mediators can create a more inclusive and effective process for resolving inheritance disputes. This cultural competence is crucial in building trust, facilitating open communication, and reaching resolutions that honor both legal requirements and cultural values.

MANAGING EMOTIONS IN INHERITANCE MEDIATION

Inheritance disputes are often laden with complex emotions - grief, anger, jealousy, and fear. Effective mediators must have strategies to address these emotions:

Grief Counseling Techniques: Incorporating elements of grief counseling can be crucial. Allowing time for siblings to share memories of the deceased can shift the focus from assets to shared loss and love.
Anger Management: When anger flares, techniques like "time-outs" or switching to individual caucuses can be effective. Teaching simple breathing exercises can also help parties regain composure.
Addressing Fear: Many inheritance disputes are driven by fear - fear of financial insecurity, fear of losing family connections, fear of dishonoring the deceased's wishes. Naming and discussing these fears openly can lead to collaborative problem-solving.
Jealousy and Resentment: These emotions often stem from long-standing family dynamics. Mediators might use genograms (family tree diagrams) to visually represent and discuss these relationships, helping parties gain perspective on ingrained patterns.

TECHNOLOGY IN MEDIATION

The digital age has transformed mediation practices:

Video Conferencing: Platforms like Zoom allow for remote mediation, crucial when family members are geographically dispersed.
Online Collaboration Tools: Shared document platforms and virtual whiteboards can facilitate real-time collaboration on agreements, even when parties aren't in the same room.
Digital Asset Division: As we saw in the O'Sullivan case in Chapter 5, digital assets like cryptocurrencies present unique challenges. Mediators now need to be versed in these technologies or bring in experts to ensure fair division.
AI and ODR: Online Dispute Resolution (ODR) platforms, some incorporating artificial intelligence, are emerging as tools for handling routine aspects of mediation, allowing human mediators to focus on more complex emotional and relational issues.

LEGAL FRAMEWORK OF MEDIATED AGREEMENTS

Understanding the legal standing of mediated agreements is crucial:

Enforceability: While mediation is generally a voluntary process, a properly drafted and signed mediated settlement agreement is typically enforceable as a contract. In some jurisdictions, these agreements can be filed with the court to gain the status of a court order.
Interaction with Existing Estate Plans: Mediated agreements must be carefully crafted to work within the constraints of existing wills or trusts. In some cases, the agreement might stipulate that parties will take legal action to modify existing estate documents.
Tax Implications: Any agreement should be reviewed by tax professionals to understand potential tax consequences, especially in cases involving large estates or complex assets.
Capacity Issues: In cases where there are concerns about a party's mental capacity, additional steps may be needed to ensure the agree-

ment is legally sound, potentially involving capacity assessments or court approval.

CONCLUSION: THE POWER OF MEDIATED SOLUTIONS

As we've seen throughout this book, inheritance disputes can tear families apart and drain estates of their value. The Johnson case demonstrates the power of mediation to not only resolve financial disagreements but also to heal familial wounds and honor the true legacy of the deceased.

Mediation negotiation, when approached with preparation, skill, and ethical integrity, offers a path to resolution that litigation often cannot provide. It allows families to move from a win-lose mentality to a win-win approach, preserving relationships and resources in the process.

As we continue our mission to stop inheritance heists, let us remember that sometimes, the best way to protect an inheritance is not through courtroom battles, but through thoughtful, structured negotiations in the mediation room. By mastering the art and science of mediation negotiation, we can help families find common ground, honor their loved ones' legacies, and move forward with renewed bonds and shared purpose.

PART TWO

CHAPTER 8
FROM HOSPITAL BED TO MEDIATION ROOM: RESOLVING INHERITANCE CONFLICTS

In the suburbs of San Jose, a family's story unfolded that would challenge the boundaries of love, law, and legacy. While the essence of this account remains true to the events that transpired, it's important to note that names and certain circumstances have been altered to preserve the privacy and anonymity of those involved. The core elements of the conflict, however, remain intact, offering valuable insights into the complexities of estate disputes and the power of mediation.

THE JANSSEN LEGACY: MISUNDERSTANDING AND RESOLUTION

At the heart of this story was Evelyn Janssen, a spirited woman in her early seventies, whose life had been full of triumphs and tribulations. Evelyn's world revolved around her two adult children: Sarah, fifty-six, a diligent accountant, and Michael, fifty-seven, whose path had taken a darker turn, leading him to a correctional facility in Southern California.

Michael's absence cast a long shadow, but his son Derek and young grandson Tyler, a bright-eyed seven-year-old, brought joy to the family. The Janssen estate, a testament to Evelyn's savvy investments, was valued at a staggering $10 million. Little did anyone know that this wealth would become the center of a storm that would test the family's bonds.

An Unexpected Turn

Life took a dramatic turn when Evelyn was rushed to the hospital. The diagnosis: a severe urinary tract infection (UTI). What seemed like a common ailment for someone her age would prove to have far-reaching consequences. As Evelyn recuperated in a rehabilitation facility, the UTI wreaked havoc on her cognitive functions. In a moment of confusion, she penned a handwritten note that would later be interpreted as her will. It read: "I, Evelyn Janssen, leave all my worldly possessions to Tylon Janssen my nephew."

This hastily scribbled document contained two critical errors. First, Tyler was Evelyn's great-grandson, not her nephew. Second, and more subtly, she had misspelled Tyler's name as "Tylon" - a mistake the usually meticulous Evelyn would never have made in her right mind.

Tragically, Evelyn passed away shortly after penning this document, leaving behind a legacy shrouded in confusion and potential conflict.

A Family Divided

The discovery of this handwritten will threw the family into turmoil. If upheld, it would mean that young Tyler—or more accurately, his guardian—would inherit the entire $10 million estate, leaving Sarah and Michael with nothing. The stakes couldn't have been higher, and the battle lines were drawn.

The Hidden Culprit: UTIs and Cognitive Impairment

Unbeknownst to many, UTIs in older adults can cause a range of neurological symptoms, often mistaken for dementia. Confusion, memory problems, and impaired judgment are just a few of the potential effects. In Evelyn's case, this UTI-induced delirium had clouded her judgment at a crucial moment, potentially altering her final wishes in ways she may never have intended.

The Path to Mediation: Seeking Common Ground

Contrary to initial assumptions, Michael's incarceration did not disqualify him from inheriting. In a surprising move, he retained the services of Hackard Law, a firm known for its expertise in complex estate litigation.

Sarah, feeling that her mother's true wishes were not reflected in the handwritten document, sought the counsel of Attorney Jacob Stern. Known in legal circles as a skilled litigator with a sterling reputation, Stern brought a wealth of experience and a measured approach to the case.

As the legal battle intensified and the costs—both financial and emotional—began to mount, all parties agreed to pursue mediation as an alternative to a lengthy and unpredictable court battle. This decision would prove to be a turning point in the Janssen family dispute.

Enter Judge Barbara Stokely: A Masterful Mediator

Retired California Superior Court Judge Barbara Stokely was brought in as the mediator. Known for her expertise in complex estate matters and her ability to navigate emotionally charged family disputes, Judge Stokely's involvement brought a new sense of hope for resolution.

"Mediation offers us the opportunity to find a solution that addresses everyone's concerns," Judge Stokely explained in the opening session. "Unlike a court verdict, mediation allows for creative solutions that can potentially preserve family relationships while respecting the intentions behind the contested will."

The Mediation Process: Unveiling Underlying Interests

Judge Stokely's approach was methodical and empathetic. She began by meeting with each party separately, allowing them to express their concerns, motivations, and desired outcomes without the pressure of direct confrontation.

Sarah, represented by Jacob Stern, emphasized her belief that the handwritten will didn't reflect her mother's true long-term intentions. "I'm not after the money," Sarah insisted. "I just want to ensure that Mom's lifetime of careful planning isn't undone by a moment of confusion."

Michael stressed the importance of honoring what could have been his mother's final wishes.

The local attorney, representing Tyler's guardian, focused on securing the young boy's future, argued for the validity of the handwritten will but expressed openness to solutions that would benefit the entire family.

Medical Testimony: A Key to Understanding

Dr. Elena Rodriguez, a geriatric specialist, provided crucial expert testimony on the effects of UTIs on elderly patients' cognitive function. This became a central point of discussion, with Judge Stokely using this information to help all parties understand the complexities of Evelyn's mental state at the time of writing the will.

"We're not here to assign blame," Judge Stokely reminded the participants. "We're here to understand the circumstances and find a solution that Evelyn would have wanted for her family."

A Marathon Session: Late Night Breakthroughs

The mediation extended into the night, with Judge Stokely tirelessly shuttling between parties, offering perspectives, and guiding discussions towards common ground. As the hours wore on, the focus shifted from winning and losing to finding a solution that could honor Evelyn's legacy and provide for the family's future.

The Settlement: A Balanced Resolution

In the early hours of the morning, after intense negotiations and emotional discussions, a settlement was reached:

- A significant trust was established for Tyler's benefit, acknowledging the intent behind Evelyn's handwritten will. However, recognizing the complexities of leaving large sums to minors, the trust was structured with careful provisions:
- A portion of the funds would be accessible for Tyler's education and healthcare needs.
- The trustee would have the power to adjust these distributions based on Tyler's maturity and circumstances.
- Portions of the estate were allocated to both Sarah and Michael, recognizing their long-standing place in Evelyn's life and previous estate plans.

This structured approach to Tyler's inheritance ensured that the young boy's future was secured while also protecting him from the potential pitfalls of receiving a large sum at a young age. It reflected a nuanced understanding of estate planning and the long-term interests of young beneficiaries.

The Aftermath: Reflection and Moving Forward

At mediation's end, the exhausted family members and their legal representatives emerged with a sense of accomplishment and relief. While the mediation hadn't erased all the hurt and mistrust that had built up, it provided a framework for the family to move forward.

LESSONS LEARNED: THE POWER OF MEDIATION IN ESTATE DISPUTES

The Janssen case became a touchstone in legal circles, highlighting the potential of mediation in resolving complex estate disputes. It demonstrated how skilled mediation could lead to nuanced solutions that court verdicts might not achieve.

A Legacy Preserved

The mediated settlement provided a foundation for potential reconciliation and a way to honor Evelyn's legacy that extended beyond mere distribution of assets.

The case served as a powerful reminder of the complexities at the intersection of aging, health, and family dynamics. It underscored the importance of clear communication, proper estate planning, and the potential for mediation to resolve even the most contentious family disputes in a way that preserves relationships and honors the true intentions of the deceased.

In the end, Judge Barbara Stokely's masterful mediation had not only resolved a legal dispute but had also allowed a legacy that honored Evelyn's life in all its complexity.

CONCLUSION

The Janssen case demonstrates the power of mediation in resolving complex inheritance disputes. As we work to stop inheritance heists, mediation offers a valuable tool for navigating family conflicts, preserving relationships, and finding creative solutions that honor the true intentions of the deceased.

CHAPTER 9
CAREGIVER CAPERS: WHEN TRUST TURNS TO TREACHERY

In the twilight years of life, many elderly individuals find themselves relying on the support and care of others. These caregivers, whether family members, friends, or professionals, often become an integral part of an elder's daily life, providing essential assistance and companionship. However, as we've seen throughout this book, the dynamics of inheritance and elder care can sometimes take a dark turn. In this chapter, we'll explore the world of "Caregiver Capers," situations where those entrusted with the care of vulnerable elders exploit their position for personal gain.

THE SCOPE OF THE PROBLEM

Before we dive into specific cases and strategies, it's crucial to understand the magnitude of caregiver exploitation. According to the National Council on Aging, approximately one in ten Americans aged sixty-plus have experienced some form of elder abuse, with some estimates ranging as high as five million elders abused each year. Financial exploitation, often perpetrated by caregivers, is one of the most common forms of elder abuse.

In California alone, Adult Protective Services (APS) receives more than 200,000 reports of elder and dependent adult abuse annually. While not all of these cases involve caregiver exploitation, a significant portion do. These statistics underscore the urgent need for awareness, prevention, and legal intervention in cases of caregiver exploitation.

DEFINING THE CAREGIVER: MORE THAN JUST A HELPER

Before we probe the potential pitfalls of caregiving relationships, it's crucial to understand what we mean by "caregiver" or "care custodian." In legal terms, a caregiver is typically defined as someone who provides assistance with daily living activities to an individual who cannot fully care for themselves due to age, illness, or disability.

California law, for instance, defines a "care custodian" in Probate Code § 21362 as:

> "A person who provides health or social services to a dependent adult, except that 'care custodian' does not include a person who provided services without remuneration if the person had a personal relationship with the dependent adult (1) at least 90 days before providing those services, (2) at least six months before the dependent adult's death, and (3) before the dependent adult was admitted to hospice care, if the dependent adult was admitted to hospice care."

This definition encompasses a wide range of individuals, from family members providing unpaid care to professional caregivers and even some healthcare providers. The breadth of this definition reflects the diverse nature of caregiving relationships and the potential for exploitation in various contexts.

THE SARAH JENSEN CASE: A CAREGIVER'S BETRAYAL

To illustrate the potential for caregiver exploitation, let's examine the case of Sarah Jensen, an eighty-seven-year-old widow living in suburban Chicago. This case, while based on real events, has been anonymized to protect privacy.

Sarah had lived independently for years after her husband's passing, but a series of small strokes left her needing daily assistance. Her children, living in different states, hired a professional caregiver named Melissa Thompson to help Sarah with daily tasks and provide companionship.

At first, Melissa seemed like a godsend. She was attentive, kind, and appeared to genuinely care for Sarah's well-being. Sarah's children were relieved to have found someone so dedicated to their mother's care.

However, things began to change subtly over time. Sarah's long-time friends reported that they found it increasingly difficult to visit or even speak with Sarah on the phone. Melissa always seemed to have an excuse for why Sarah couldn't come to the phone or why visits weren't convenient.

Sarah's children also noticed changes in their mother's financial situation. Large withdrawals were being made from her accounts, ostensibly for household expenses and medical bills. When questioned, Melissa always had plausible explanations, backed up by a flurry of receipts and invoices.

The situation came to a head when Sarah's daughter Lisa made a surprise visit. She found her mother looking unkempt and confused, living in a house that was far from the immaculate home Sarah had always maintained. More alarmingly, Lisa discovered that Melissa had convinced Sarah to change her will, leaving a substantial portion of her estate to Melissa.

Upon investigation, it was revealed that Melissa had systematically isolated Sarah from her friends and family, exerting undue influence to gain control of her finances and alter her estate plans. Over the course of two years, Melissa had siphoned off over $300,000 from Sarah's accounts and had positioned herself to inherit a significant portion of Sarah's $1.2 million estate.

This case highlights several key aspects of caregiver exploitation:

- Isolation of the elderly person from friends and family
- Gradual assumption of control over finances
- Manipulation of estate planning documents

- Exploitation of the elder's trust and vulnerability

THE MECHANICS OF UNDUE INFLUENCE IN CAREGIVING

The Sarah Jensen case illustrates how caregivers can exert undue influence over their charges. Undue influence, as we've discussed in previous chapters, occurs when someone uses their position of trust or authority to override the free will of another person, typically for personal gain.

In the context of caregiving, undue influence often follows a predictable pattern:

1. Isolation: The caregiver gradually limits the elder's contact with friends and family, often under the guise of protecting the elder's health or privacy.
2. Dependency: The caregiver fosters a sense of dependency, making the elder feel that they cannot manage without the caregiver's constant presence and assistance.
3. Manipulation: The caregiver uses various tactics to manipulate the elder's emotions and decision-making, often playing on fears of abandonment or financial insecurity.
4. Financial Control: The caregiver gradually assumes control over the elder's finances, often starting with small tasks like bill paying and progressing to larger financial decisions.
5. Estate Planning Changes: Finally, the caregiver may pressure the elder to change their will, trust, or other estate planning documents to benefit the caregiver.

GRIEF AND VULNERABILITY IN CAREGIVING RELATIONSHIPS

As we navigate the complex landscape of caregiver relationships, it's crucial to understand the role that grief plays in making elders more vulnerable to exploitation. Grief, whether from the loss of a spouse, declining health, or the gradual loss of independence, can significantly impact an elder's emotional state and decision-making capacity. This vulnerability, coupled with the intimate nature of caregiving relationships, can create a perfect storm for potential exploitation.

How Grief Makes Elders More Susceptible to Exploitation

Emotional Vulnerability: Grief often leaves elders feeling emotionally raw and seeking comfort. This emotional vulnerability can make them more susceptible to manipulation by unscrupulous caregivers who may exploit their need for emotional support.
Cognitive Impairment: Grief can temporarily impair cognitive function, affecting judgment and decision-making abilities. This can make it easier for caregivers to influence financial decisions or changes to estate plans.
Isolation: Grieving elders may withdraw from social interactions, increasing their isolation and dependence on caregivers. This isolation can provide more opportunities for exploitation and make it harder for family members to detect issues.
Desire for Connection: The loss of a long-term partner or friends can leave elders craving companionship. Caregivers may exploit this need, positioning themselves as the elder's primary emotional support and using this connection to gain undue influence.
Financial Vulnerability: Grief can lead to apathy about financial matters, especially if the deceased spouse previously handled finances. This disengagement can create opportunities for financial exploitation by caregivers.

THE CASE OF ELEANOR AND JAMES

Consider the case of Eleanor, an eighty-two-year-old widow who lost her husband of sixty years, James. In the months following James's death, Eleanor's grief was profound. Her daughter Sarah hired a caregiver named Lisa to help Eleanor with daily tasks and provide companionship.

Initially, Lisa seemed to be a source of comfort for Eleanor. However, Sarah began to notice changes:

- Eleanor became increasingly dependent on Lisa, often deferring to her on decisions James would have previously made.
- Lisa began to suggest changes to Eleanor's financial arrangements, citing conversations she claimed to have had with Eleanor about her wishes.
- Eleanor's other relationships, including with her grandchildren, seemed to take a backseat to her relationship with Lisa.

This case illustrates how grief can create a vulnerability that caregivers might exploit, blurring the lines between appropriate care and undue influence.

COMPLEX EMOTIONS FOR FAMILY MEMBERS

When family members suspect a caregiver of exploitation, they often experience a complex mix of emotions:

Guilt: Family members may feel guilty for not being able to provide care themselves, leading to self-doubt when suspicions arise.
Anger: The betrayal of trust by a caregiver can evoke intense anger, both at the caregiver and at themselves for not detecting the exploitation sooner.
Confusion: The gradual nature of many exploitation scenarios can leave family members questioning their own perceptions and wondering if they're overreacting.
Fear: There's often fear about confronting the situation – fear of being wrong, fear of upsetting the elder, and fear of potential retaliation by the caregiver.
Grief: Family members may experience their own sense of grief, mourning the loss of trust and the impact on their relationship with the elder.
Helplessness: The complexity of elder exploitation cases can leave family members feeling powerless, especially if the elder denies any wrongdoing by the caregiver.

Navigating these emotions while trying to protect a vulnerable loved one can be overwhelming for family members. It's crucial for legal professionals to recognize and address these emotional challenges when working with families suspecting caregiver exploitation.

Strategies for Addressing Grief-Related Vulnerability

Grief Counseling: Encourage elders to seek grief counseling or join support groups to process their loss in a healthy way.
Family Involvement: Maintain regular family involvement in the elder's life, even when a caregiver is present, to provide emotional support and oversight.
Financial Safeguards: Implement financial safeguards, such as requiring two signatures on large transactions, to protect against impulsive decisions made during periods of grief.
Regular Check-ins: Establish a system of regular check-ins with the elder, involving multiple family members or trusted friends to create a network of support and oversight.
Professional Oversight: Consider engaging a professional care manager or fiduciary to provide an additional layer of oversight in caregiving relationships.
Education: Educate family members about the signs of exploitation and the increased vulnerability that can come with grief.

Understanding the intersection of grief and vulnerability in caregiving relationships is crucial in our efforts to prevent and address caregiver exploitation. By recognizing how grief can make elders more susceptible to manipulation and acknowledging the complex emotions family members face when suspecting exploitation, we can develop more effective strategies for protecting vulnerable elders and supporting their families.

As legal professionals, it's our responsibility to approach these cases with sensitivity to the emotional dynamics at play, while still vigorously advocating for the rights and well-being of vulnerable elders. By doing so, we can help ensure that caregiving relationships remain sources of support and comfort, rather than avenues for exploitation.

THE "FREEZE OUT": ISOLATING ELDERS FROM FAMILY

One of the most insidious tactics used by exploitative caregivers is the "freeze out" - systematically isolating the elder from their family and longtime friends. This isolation serves several purposes:

- It reduces the chances of the exploitation being discovered.
- It increases the elder's dependence on the caregiver.
- It allows the caregiver to control the narrative about the elder's condition and needs.

The freeze out often begins subtly. The caregiver might screen phone calls, claiming the elder is resting or not feeling well enough to talk. Visits from family and friends are discouraged, with the caregiver citing concerns about the elder's health or energy levels.

Over time, the elder becomes increasingly isolated, with the caregiver becoming their primary or sole point of contact with the outside world. This isolation makes it easier for the caregiver to exert undue influence and harder for family members to intervene.

THE GONZALES FAMILY DILEMMA: WHEN FAMILY CAREGIVERS EXPLOIT

While many cases of caregiver exploitation involve professional caregivers, it's important to recognize that family members acting as caregivers can also engage in exploitative behavior. The case of the Gonzales family illustrates this painful reality.

Maria Gonzales, seventy-nine, had been diagnosed with early-stage Alzheimer's disease. Her three children - Carlos, Elena, and Miguel - agreed that she needed full-time care. Elena, who was between jobs, volunteered to move in with their mother and become her primary caregiver.

At first, the arrangement seemed ideal. Elena provided loving care, and Maria appeared to be thriving in her familiar home environment. However, Carlos and Miguel began to notice troubling signs:

- Elena became increasingly resistant to their visits, always finding reasons why it wasn't a good time to see their mother.
- When they did visit, Maria seemed withdrawn and anxious, especially when Elena was present.
- Large purchases were being made using Maria's credit cards, including a new car registered in Elena's name.
- Maria's longtime friends reported that Elena had told them visits were no longer welcome as they "upset" Maria.

The situation came to a head when Carlos and Miguel discovered that Elena had taken their mother to a lawyer to revise her will, leaving the bulk of the estate to Elena and significantly reducing Carlos and Miguel's inheritances.

This case highlights the complex dynamics that can arise when family members become caregivers. The trust and authority granted to a family caregiver can sometimes be abused, leading to financial exploitation and the manipulation of estate plans.

LEGAL SAFEGUARDS AND RED FLAGS

Given the potential for caregiver exploitation, it's crucial for families and legal professionals to be aware of the safeguards available and the red flags that may indicate exploitation is occurring.

Legal Safeguards:

Power of Attorney Limitations: Ensure that powers of attorney have appropriate limitations and oversight mechanisms.
Professional Fiduciaries: Consider appointing a professional fiduciary to manage finances, rather than relying solely on a caregiver.

Regular Accounting: Require regular accounting of all financial transactions made on behalf of the elder.
Visitation Rights: Establish clear visitation rights for family members in any caregiving agreement.

Red Flags:

- Sudden changes in estate planning documents, especially those that benefit the caregiver.
- Unexplained financial transactions or changes in financial management.
- Isolation from family and friends, particularly if the elder previously enjoyed an active social life.
- Signs of neglect or substandard care, despite the caregiver having access to sufficient funds.
- The caregiver's reluctance to provide information about the elder's condition or finances.

PROSECUTIONS OF CAREGIVER FINANCIAL EXPLOITATION

In recent years, there has been an increasing focus on prosecuting caregivers who financially exploit vulnerable elders. Several high-profile cases illustrate the seriousness with which authorities are treating these crimes:

In 2022, California caregiver Heidi Miller was sentenced to four years in prison for stealing over $500,000 from an elderly couple she was caring for. Miller abused her position of trust to access the couple's financial accounts and make unauthorized purchases and withdrawals over several years.

Florida caregiver Odalis Lopez received a fifty-one-month prison sentence in 2021 for exploiting an elderly Holocaust survivor and his wife. Lopez stole over $100,000 from the couple by using their credit cards for personal purchases while working as their home health aide.

In New York in 2020, caregiver Stephany Hernandez was charged with grand larceny for allegedly stealing over $100,000 from an eighty-nine-year-old woman she was hired to assist. Hernandez allegedly used the victim's credit cards and bank accounts for her own benefit.

Massachusetts caregiver Mariana Batista was indicted in 2019 for allegedly stealing more than $120,000 from an elderly disabled woman. Batista allegedly wrote checks to herself from the victim's account and made ATM withdrawals for personal use.

In 2018, Illinois caregiver Joyce Mahoney received a four-year prison sentence for financially exploiting an eighty-eight-year-old woman with dementia. Mahoney stole over $35,000 from the victim by writing checks to herself and making unauthorized purchases.

These cases demonstrate the growing awareness of caregiver financial exploitation and the willingness of prosecutors to pursue charges against those who take advantage of vulnerable elders.

PREVENTION STRATEGIES: SAFEGUARDING AGAINST CAREGIVER EXPLOITATION

As we've emphasized throughout this book, prevention is often the best strategy when it comes to inheritance disputes and elder exploitation. Here are some key prevention strategies to consider:

Regular Family Check-ins: Establish a system of regular family meetings or check-ins to discuss the elder's care and financial situation. This can help prevent isolation and catch potential issues early.
Professional Oversight: Consider engaging a professional fiduciary or care manager to oversee the caregiver's activities and the elder's finances.
Clear Documentation: Ensure that all financial transactions and care decisions are clearly documented. This can help prevent disputes and provide evidence if exploitation is suspected.
Education: Educate family members and the elder about the signs of financial exploitation and undue influence. Knowledge is a powerful preventive tool.
Estate Planning Safeguards: Work with an experienced estate planning attorney to build safeguards into estate documents. This might

include provisions for third-party oversight or restrictions on changes to estate plans.

Background Checks: Always conduct thorough background checks on potential caregivers, whether they're professionals or family members taking on the role.

Open Communication: Foster an environment of open communication within the family. As we saw in Chapter 3 with the White family, open dialogue can prevent misunderstandings and conflicts.

LEGAL REMEDIES FOR CAREGIVER EXPLOITATION

When prevention fails and exploitation occurs, legal remedies become necessary. In California, several legal avenues are available:

Elder Abuse Litigation: Under the Elder Abuse and Dependent Adult Civil Protection Act, victims or their families can sue for damages, including pain and suffering.

Undue Influence Claims: As discussed in earlier chapters, undue influence can be grounds for invalidating changes to wills or trusts.

Conservatorship: In cases where the elder is no longer able to manage their own affairs, a conservatorship may be necessary to protect their interests.

Criminal Prosecution: In severe cases, financial elder abuse can lead to criminal charges against the perpetrator.

Trust Contests: Trust contests can be initiated to challenge trust provisions that may have resulted from caregiver exploitation.

HACKARD LAW: EXPERIENCED FIGHTERS AGAINST CAREGIVER EXPLOITATION

As the founder of Hackard Law and author of this book, I've seen firsthand the devastating impact of caregiver abuse on vulnerable seniors and their families. Over the years, our firm has successfully litigated dozens of cases that share disturbing patterns of exploitation.

One case that stands out involved an elderly client we'll call Robert, a seventy-year-old retired teacher. Robert's children came to us when they noticed their father's declining health coincided with his caregiver gaining control over his affairs.

The caregiver had somehow become the primary beneficiary of Robert's trust, effectively disinheriting his children. It was a classic case of undue influence, and we were determined to set things right.

Another memorable case involved Margaret, a seventy-five-year-old woman in the early stages of Alzheimer's. Her caregivers, a married couple, had manipulated her into transferring her vacation home to them. When Margaret's son came to us, he was distressed to find his mother isolated, confused, and living in poor conditions. Through our efforts, we were able to invalidate the property transfer and remove the exploitative caregivers.

At Hackard Law, we've developed strategies to combat these "Caregiver Capers." Our approach typically involves:

- Thorough investigation to uncover evidence of undue influence or financial exploitation
- Collaboration with forensic accountants to trace misappropriated funds
- Use of geriatric psychiatrists to establish the elder's mental state and vulnerability to exploitation
- Aggressive litigation to invalidate fraudulent transfers and estate plan changes

Our successes in cases like these send a clear message: unscrupulous caregivers will be held accountable. But more importantly, they offer hope to families facing similar situations. We're committed to being a voice for those who can no longer speak for themselves, ensuring that seniors' rights and wishes are respected and protected.

The fight against elder abuse is ongoing, but I'm proud of the work we do at Hackard Law. It's not just about legal victories - it's about preserving dignity, honoring legacies, and protecting the vulnerable. That's what drives me and our team every single day.

CONCLUSION

In this chapter, we've explored the critical issue of caregiver exploitation, a form of inheritance heist that preys on some of society's most vulnerable members. We've seen how caregivers, entrusted with the well-being of elders, can sometimes betray that trust for personal gain. Key takeaways include:

- The prevalence and scope of caregiver exploitation
- The mechanics of undue influence in caregiving relationships
- The importance of prevention strategies, including regular family check-ins and professional oversight
- Legal remedies available when exploitation occurs

As we continue our mission to stop inheritance heists, vigilance against caregiver exploitation is crucial. By understanding the signs, implementing prevention strategies, and knowing when to seek legal help, we can better protect our elders and preserve their legacies.

CHAPTER 10
THE DIGITAL FRONTIER: NAVIGATING CRYPTOCURRENCY LITIGATION AND ESTATE PLANNING

In the sun-soaked streets of Miami, far from the tech hubs of Silicon Valley, Eileen and Robert O'Sullivan found themselves thrust into a world they barely understood. Their son James, known to friends and family as Jimmy, had built a life for himself in California's Silicon Beach, becoming a legend in the cryptocurrency world. But Jimmy's untimely and unexpected death at the age of thirty-nine would set in motion a series of events that would challenge the very foundations of inheritance law and force the legal system to grapple with questions it was ill-prepared to answer.

THE NEW WILD WEST OF INHERITANCE

Jimmy, a brilliant software engineer who had worked for tech giants like Google, Facebook, and Twitter, had amassed a fortune in various cryptocurrencies. His portfolio, as his parents would later discover, was worth over $40 million - a testament to his foresight and technical acumen. But as is often the case, even the most brilliant minds can overlook the crucial details of estate planning.

This chapter explores the O'Sullivan family's journey through the complexities of cryptocurrency inheritance, the potential pitfalls of digital asset estate planning, and the emerging legal frameworks attempting to bring order to this digital wild west. Their tale serves as a cautionary reminder that in the world of inheritance, innovation often outpaces legislation, leaving families to navigate uncharted waters.

THE O'SULLIVAN LEGACY: A HIDDEN DIGITAL FORTUNE

Jimmy O'Sullivan's rise in the tech world was meteoric. Starting as a software engineer at major tech companies, he quickly recognized the potential of blockchain technology and cryptocurrencies. In 2013, Jimmy began investing in various cryptocurrencies, building a diverse portfolio that included:

- Bitcoin (BTC)
- Ethereum (ETH)
- And various altcoins and NFTs

What made Jimmy's digital fortune unique was not just its decentralized nature, but its complete invisibility to his family. Unlike traditional assets held by banks or brokerages, his cryptocurrency was stored across multiple hardware wallets, some in cold storage, others in various online exchanges. This decentralization and secrecy, while offering privacy during his life, would soon become a significant hurdle for his family.

Tragically, Jimmy's death came without warning, leaving his affairs in disarray. He had not prepared a will, and crucially, he had not left any information about the existence of his cryptocurrency holdings. This oversight would prove to be the catalyst for a complex legal battle that would expose the vulnerabilities in current estate law when dealing with digital assets.

The Crypto Conundrum: When Access is Everything

Jimmy's sudden death left his family reeling. As Eileen and Robert grappled with their loss from their home in Florida, they soon faced a stark reality: they had no idea about the extent of Jimmy's assets, let alone how to access them and manage them if they did access them.

The challenges they faced were numerous:

Unknown assets: Jimmy had not left any record of his cryptocurrency investments, leaving his parents unaware of the fortune he had accumulated.
Multiple wallets, unknown passwords: Even if they knew about the cryptocurrencies, Jimmy had used various hardware wallets to store them, each protected by complex passwords and seed phrases. Without these, the funds were essentially locked away forever.
Two-factor authentication: Many of Jimmy's exchange accounts were secured with two-factor authentication tied to his personal devices, which were now inaccessible.
Lack of inventory: Jimmy had not left a comprehensive inventory of his digital assets, making it difficult to even know the full extent of his holdings.
Jurisdictional issues: With Jimmy's parents in Florida and his assets in California, questions of jurisdiction further complicated the matter.

As the family grappled with these issues, they quickly realized that without access, Jimmy's digital fortune might as well not exist at all. This scenario starkly contrasted with more traditional inheritance challenges, where the assets themselves were rarely in question, only their distribution.

The Unexpected Administrator: A Stepbrother's Role

In a twist that would later prove fateful, the court appointed Seamus Flynn, a distant cousin of Jimmy, as the administrator of Jimmy's estate. Seamus lived near Jimmy and he indicated that he had some familiarity with cryptocurrency. Lacking counsel and not knowing any other options, Jimmy's parents nominated Seamus to become the administrator of Jimmy's estate. He was granted full authority to administer the estate under the Independent Administration of Estates Act.

Initially, Seamus's appointment seemed like a stroke of luck. Living in California, he was better positioned to handle Jimmy's affairs than his Florida-based cousins. Seamus presented himself as eager to help, promising to leave no stone unturned in his search for Jimmy's assets.

This appointment gave Seamus access to Jimmy's digital footprint, including his email accounts and personal devices.

From early, 2021, Seamus had access to Jimmy's personal email mailbox, providing him with crucial information about Jimmy's cryptocurrency holdings.

The Unraveling of a Digital Fortune

Over the next two years, a complex and troubling scenario unfolded. Seamus, as the estate administrator, took control of Jimmy's cryptocurrency assets. However, the full extent of these digital holdings remained shrouded in mystery.

Seamus's filings with the probate court painted an incomplete picture. He reported only a fraction of the assets, claiming a total estate value far below its actual worth. In reality, Jimmy's Coinbase account alone held:

- More than 400 Bitcoin (worth approximately $20 million at the time)
- At least 3,000 Ethereum (worth approximately $12 million at the time)

During this period, Seamus did distribute some of the cryptocurrency assets to Jimmy's parents, Eileen and Robert. He repeatedly promised to distribute the remainder, assuring them that he was acting in the best interests of the estate. However, as time passed, these promises remained unfulfilled, and the bulk of the digital fortune remained unaccounted for.

The Legal Labyrinth: Cryptocurrency and Probate Law

The O'Sullivan case highlighted the complex legal landscape surrounding cryptocurrency and probate law. The challenges were multifaceted:

Asset classification: How should cryptocurrencies be classified for estate purposes? Are they currency, securities, or a new asset class entirely?
Jurisdiction: With decentralized assets stored on global networks, which jurisdiction's laws apply? The complexity was compounded by Jimmy's parents living in Florida while his assets were primarily in California.
Valuation: How to value highly volatile digital assets for estate tax purposes?
Privacy vs. Disclosure: How to balance the need for privacy in crypto transactions with the disclosure requirements of probate?
These challenges underscored the need for flexibility in estate planning. The static nature of traditional wills and trusts is ill-suited to the dynamic world of digital assets.

THE HUNT FOR DIGITAL KEYS: A FAMILY'S QUEST

As the legal complexities unfolded, Eileen and Robert embarked on a desperate search for any information that might help them access Jimmy's digital fortune. This quest paralleled other cases where family members were left in the dark about crucial financial information.

They scoured Jimmy's personal effects, looking for any notes or clues that might lead to passwords or seed phrases. They examined:

- Books for annotations or hidden notes
- Family photos for potential coded messages
- Jimmy's collection of vintage video games for clues

Their search yielded tantalizing fragments:

- A cryptic note in Jimmy's day planner: "Remember 2-6-4. Key to everything."

- A series of seemingly random words scribbled on the back of an old receipt
- A USB drive containing encrypted files that no one could access

But with each potential breakthrough came new frustrations. Every apparent clue led to more questions than answers.

The Unfolding Drama: Suspicions and Legal Action

Two years after Seamus's appointment as administrator, Eileen and Robert's growing concerns led them to seek legal counsel. It was at this point that they reached out to Hackard Law to investigate the matter and, if necessary, litigate for the recovery of the undistributed assets.

As the investigation into Jimmy's estate began, several alarming red flags emerged:

Undisclosed Assets: Seamus's filings with the probate court failed to mention the full extent of Jimmy's cryptocurrency holdings.
Partial Distributions: While some assets had been distributed to the parents, a significant portion remained unaccounted for.
Unfulfilled Promises: Despite repeated assurances, Seamus had failed to distribute the remainder of the assets as promised.
Mysterious Transfers: The initial investigation uncovered evidence that large sums of cryptocurrencies had been moved from Jimmy's accounts after his death.
Sudden Wealth: Seamus, who had previously been in financial difficulties, suddenly seemed flush with cash. Most notably, he had used several million dollars to finance a high-end sports car collection - a lifelong dream that had mysteriously become reality.

Recognizing the complexity of this case, Hackard Law assembled a team with diverse expertise. They brought on Sam Collins, a highly regarded retired detective, whose investigative skills would prove invaluable in unraveling the web of digital transactions. Additionally, they enlisted the help of Pat O'Brien, a seasoned trial litigator with extensive experience in both federal and state law enforcement prosecution. Their combined expertise in digital forensics and high-stakes litigation would be crucial in building the case.

With this team in place, Hackard Law filed a lawsuit against Seamus on behalf of Eileen and Robert, alleging financial elder abuse, breach of fiduciary duty, and fraud. This legal action marked the beginning of efforts to recover the misappropriated digital assets and hold Seamus accountable for his actions as estate administrator.

The Legal Battle Unfolds

The lawsuit brought by Eileen and Robert against Seamus revealed the extent of the alleged fraud:

Missing Cryptocurrencies: The suit claimed that significant amounts of Bitcoin and Ethereum were unaccounted for, worth millions of dollars.
Fraudulent Conveyance: The transfer of newly acquired property and the investment in the car collection were alleged to be attempts to launder the stolen cryptocurrency and avoid liability.
Breach of Fiduciary Duty: Seamus was accused of breaching his duty by misrepresenting the extent of Jimmy's cryptocurrency assets to the probate court and misappropriating assets for personal use.

Recognizing the urgent need to prevent further dissipation of assets, Hackard Law took swift and strategic action. Brian Geremia and Dave Jones, both invaluable members of the team, worked tirelessly to secure court orders directing various cryptocurrency exchanges to freeze assets associated with Seamus and the estate. This move, while complex due to the decentralized nature of cryptocurrency, proved crucial in halting the outflow of digital assets.

Sam Collins's investigative expertise was instrumental in tracing the complex web of cryptocurrency transactions. His meticulous work provided the foundation for the legal arguments and helped identify hidden assets that might otherwise have gone unnoticed.

Pat O'Brien's prosecution background proved invaluable in

building a compelling case that could withstand scrutiny in both criminal and civil contexts. His expertise in handling complex financial crimes added a layer of depth to the legal strategy that would prove crucial as the case unfolded.

The team's persistence paid off. Through meticulous tracing of asset transfers and strategic use of the court's authority, they were able to recover several million dollars' worth of cryptocurrency. A breakthrough came during a mediation session, where the pressure of mounting evidence led to the revelation of additional asset locations.

However, the case is far from over. The search for additional cryptocurrency assets continues, with forensic experts combing through blockchain transactions and digital footprints. This ongoing investigation underscores the complexity of digital asset recovery and the need for specialized expertise in handling cryptocurrency-related estate disputes.

LESSONS LEARNED: A NEW APPROACH TO DIGITAL ESTATE PLANNING

The O'Sullivan case became a watershed moment in the world of digital asset estate planning. It highlighted the urgent need for individuals and legal professionals to adapt to the realities of cryptocurrency.

Key takeaways included:

Comprehensive Digital Asset Inventory: The importance of maintaining a secure, up-to-date inventory of all digital assets, including access information.
Clear Succession Planning: Establishing clear protocols for how digital assets should be handled after death, including who should have access and how they should be distributed.
Regular Updates: The need to regularly review and update digital asset plans to keep pace with technological changes and new acquisitions.
Education: The importance of educating heirs about how to access and manage digital assets.

Balancing Security and Accessibility: Developing strategies that maintain the security of digital assets during life while ensuring they remain accessible to heirs.

Legal Framework Adaptation: The need for legal systems to evolve to better address the unique characteristics of digital assets in estate planning and probate.

CONCLUSION: EMBRACING THE FUTURE OF INHERITANCE

As the O'Sullivan case continues to unfold, it's clear that the intersection of digital assets and estate law is a new frontier in inheritance disputes. The family's journey through the complexities of cryptocurrency inheritance serves as both a cautionary tale and a beacon for the future.

In the quest to stop inheritance heists, we must now contend not just with traditional threats, but with the unique challenges posed by digital assets. The immutability and decentralization that make cryptocurrencies attractive also create new pitfalls for the unprepared.

As we move forward, it's crucial that individuals, legal professionals, and lawmakers work together to create a framework that honors the innovative spirit of digital assets while protecting the rights and interests of heirs. By embracing the lessons learned from cases like the O'Sullivan's, we can ensure that the treasures of the virtual world, like those of the physical world, can be passed on securely and meaningfully to future generations.

The lessons being learned and the strategies being developed will undoubtedly shape the future of estate planning and probate law in the digital age. As legal professionals, we must remain vigilant, adaptable, and innovative in our approach to these new challenges, always striving to protect our clients' interests in an ever-evolving digital landscape.

CHAPTER 11
BLENDED FAMILIES AND INHERITANCE: BALANCING COMPETING INTERESTS

THE MODERN FAMILY DILEMMA

In modern American life, blended families have become increasingly common and significant. Recent statistics paint a clear picture of this trend:

- According to the most recent data from Pew Research Center, 16% of children are living in blended families - defined as a household with a stepparent, step-sibling, or half-sibling.
- The U.S. Bureau of Census reports that 1,300 new stepfamilies are formed each day.
- Over 40% of U.S. families are now blended families, according to recent estimates.
- It is estimated that more than half of all Americans have either been, or will be included in a blended family during their lifetime.

These families, born from remarriage or new partnerships, bring joy and companionship but also present unique challenges when it comes to estate planning and inheritance. As we've seen throughout this book, inheritance disputes can tear apart even the most harmonious families. When step-parents, step-siblings, and half-siblings are involved, the potential for conflict multiplies exponentially.

The changing landscape of American families further complicates these issues:

- The share of children living in a two-parent household is at the lowest point in more than half a century: 69% are in this type of family arrangement today, compared with 73% in 2000 and 87% in 1960.
- Fully 62% of children live with two married parents – an all-time low. Some 15% are living with parents in a remarriage and 7% are living with parents who are cohabiting.
- The share of children living with one parent stands at 26%, up from 22% in 2000 and just 9% in 1960.

And while the term "blended family" is modern, the concept is not new. The Bible offers several examples of complex family structures and the challenges they face: Abraham, Jacob, and David offer reminders that blended families have faced challenges throughout history. They also offer wisdom on how to navigate these complexities:

> "But if anyone does not provide for his relatives, and especially for members of his household, he has denied the faith and is worse than an unbeliever" (1 Timothy 5:8).

This chapter explores the delicate balance required to navigate inheritance issues in blended families, drawing on biblical wisdom, legal expertise, and real-world case studies to provide guidance for those facing this complex situation.

THE MARTINEZ-THOMPSON CASE: A BLENDED FAMILY INHERITANCE DISPUTE

To illustrate the challenges blended families face in inheritance matters, let's examine the case of the Martinez-Thompson family.

While the names and specific details have been changed to protect privacy, the core elements of this case are based on real events that unfolded in a Southern California probate court.

Carlos Martinez, a successful restaurateur, married Susan Thompson in 2010. It was a second marriage for both. Carlos had two adult children from his first marriage: Elena (35) and Miguel (32); Susan had one adult daughter from her previous marriage: Jessica (28).

Together, Carlos and Susan had a daughter, Sofia, born in 2012.

Carlos, wanting to provide for his new family while also ensuring his older children were taken care of, created a trust in 2015. The trust stipulated that:

- The family home would go to Susan.
- His restaurant business would be divided equally between Elena and Miguel.
- A college fund was set up for Sofia.
- The remainder of his assets would be divided equally among all four children.

Carlos passed away unexpectedly in 2022. What seemed like a clear and fair estate plan quickly unraveled into a complex legal battle. Elena and Miguel felt that Susan had unduly influenced their father to leave her the family home, which had significantly appreciated in value. Jessica, while named as an equal beneficiary of the remaining assets, felt excluded from the more valuable restaurant business. Susan argued that she needed the home to raise Sofia and that the college fund was insufficient given the rising costs of education.

This case highlights several key issues common in blended family inheritance disputes:

- Perceived favoritism towards the new spouse or younger children
- Step-siblings feeling excluded from family business assets
- Conflicting needs between providing for a new spouse and children from previous marriages

- The challenge of equitable distribution when assets have different emotional and financial values

REAL-WORLD COMPLEXITIES: THE HAROLD AND VIVIAN CASE

Another particularly striking case that illustrate the complexities of blended family inheritance disputes involves Harold, a wealthy entrepreneur, and his second wife, Vivian. This case exemplifies how vulnerable elderly individuals can be to manipulation and how quickly a seemingly solid estate plan can unravel.

Case Study: Harold's Manipulated Trust

Harold, a seventy-seven-year-old widower, had four adult children from his first marriage to Eleanor, who had passed away from cancer at seventy-two. Harold's life took an unexpected turn when Vivian, a woman he didn't know and who was the same age as his oldest daughter, appeared at his doorstep. Claiming to be from his church, Vivian quickly insinuated herself into Harold's life, eventually marrying him and taking control of his household.

The sequence of events that followed raised several red flags:

Sale of Family Assets: Harold and Vivian sold the family home, purchasing a smaller home in San Jose and an additional property in Lake Tahoe. This move effectively displaced the family's emotional connection to their longtime home.

Trust Modification: Harold revised his family trust, providing for:

- $900,000 in lump sum payments to be split among his children upon his death.
- Vivian to become the surviving trustee.
- Income to be paid to Vivian during her lifetime.

- The remainder to be distributed to Harold's children upon Vivian's death.

Misappropriation of Assets: After Harold's death in 2010, Vivian's actions became increasingly problematic:

- She diverted maturing bond proceeds (over $2.5 million) from the trust into her personal accounts.
- She set up pet trusts for her dogs.
- When the Lake Tahoe home sold for $1.5 million, she again redirected the funds to her personal account.
- She informed Harold's children in 2024 that the trust was depleted, and they would receive nothing.

This case highlights several critical issues we often encounter in blended family inheritance disputes:

Vulnerability of Elderly Individuals: Harold's case demonstrates how quickly a newcomer can influence an elderly person's decision-making, especially following the loss of a long-term spouse and the ensuing grief of the survivor.

The Importance of Trustee Oversight: Vivian's ability to misappropriate funds underscores the need for checks and balances in trust administration, especially when the trustee is a beneficiary. The Trust was managed or mismanaged by by Vivian from the time of Harold's death until her disclosure to his children in 2024 that everything was gone.

The Challenge of Proving Undue Influence: While Vivian's actions post-death were clearly inappropriate, proving that she unduly influenced Harold in modifying his trust can be complex and often requires forensic financial investigation. Moreover, the time for a trust challenge based on undue influence is long gone.

The Role of Clear Communication: Had Harold openly discussed his estate plans with his children, they might have been able to raise concerns or seek protections before his passing.

The Need for Professional Advice: This case underscores the importance of seeking independent legal and financial advice when making significant changes to estate plans, especially in the context of a new marriage.

When Harold's children sought advice from Hackard Law in 2024, we recognized the hallmarks of financial elder abuse and breach of fiduciary duty. Our approach in such cases typically involves:

- Thorough forensic accounting to trace misappropriated funds.
- Gathering evidence of undue influence, including timeline analysis and witness interviews.
- Pursuing legal action to remove the trustee and recover misappropriated assets.
- Seeking to invalidate trust modifications made under suspicious circumstances.

This case serves as a stark reminder of the vulnerabilities that can arise in blended family situations, especially when significant wealth is involved. It underscores the need for robust estate planning, clear communication, and vigilant oversight to protect the interests of all family members.

LEGAL CHALLENGES IN BLENDED FAMILY INHERITANCES

The Martinez-Thompson case illustrates several legal challenges that are common in blended family inheritance disputes:

Competing Spousal Rights: In many states, spouses have certain rights to inheritance that can conflict with provisions for children from previous marriages.
Undue Influence Claims: As in the Martinez-Thompson case, children from previous marriages may claim that the new spouse exerted undue influence over the deceased parent.
Community Property vs. Separate Property: In community property

states like California, distinguishing between assets acquired before and during the new marriage can be complex.

Trust Interpretation: Ambiguities in trust language can lead to disputes over the intended distribution of assets.

Fiduciary Duty Conflicts: When a surviving spouse is named as trustee, they may face conflicts between their personal interests and their fiduciary duty to all beneficiaries.

STRATEGIES FOR BLENDED FAMILY ESTATE PLANNING

To avoid the pitfalls illustrated in the Martinez-Thompson case, consider the following strategies:

Clear Communication: As we discussed, open dialogue about estate plans is crucial. In blended families, this may include family meetings with all adult children and spouses.

Detailed, Unambiguous Estate Plans: Clear and specific language in wills and trusts is essential. In blended families, this clarity becomes even more critical.

Consider a QTIP Trust: A Qualified Terminable Interest Property (QTIP) trust can provide for a surviving spouse while ensuring that assets ultimately pass to chosen beneficiaries (often children from a previous marriage).

Use of Life Insurance: Life insurance can be used to provide for a new spouse without diminishing the inheritance of children from previous marriages.

Prenuptial and Postnuptial Agreements: These agreements can clarify financial arrangements and inheritance plans in blended families.

Regular Reviews and Updates: As family dynamics change, regular reviews of estate plans are crucial.

Professional Trustee: Consider appointing a professional trustee to manage complex blended family trusts, avoiding potential conflicts of interest.

MEDIATION IN BLENDED FAMILY DISPUTES

As we explored, mediation can be a powerful tool for resolving inheritance disputes. In blended family situations, mediation offers several advantages:

Preserving Relationships: Mediation can help maintain family bonds that might be irreparably damaged by litigation.
Addressing Emotional Aspects: A skilled mediator can help family members work through the complex emotions often present in blended family disputes.
Creative Solutions: Mediation allows for more flexible and creative solutions than a court might provide.
Privacy: Unlike court proceedings, mediation keeps family matters private.

In the Martinez-Thompson case, had the family opted for mediation, they might have reached a solution that addressed everyone's concerns without the bitterness of a court battle. For instance, a mediator might have helped them explore options like:

- Selling the family home and dividing the proceeds
- Creating a buy-out agreement for the restaurant business
- Establishing a family foundation that benefits all children equally

THE EMOTIONAL LANDSCAPE OF BLENDED FAMILY INHERITANCE

The emotional aspects of inheritance disputes can be profound. In blended families, these emotions are often intensified by:

- Feelings of loyalty to biological parents
- Fear of being displaced by step-siblings
- Grief complicated by complex family dynamics
- Resentment over perceived favoritism

Understanding and addressing these emotions is crucial for both estate planning and dispute resolution in blended families.

CONCLUSION: HONORING ALL FAMILY BONDS

Navigating inheritance issues in blended families requires a delicate balance of legal acumen, emotional intelligence, and ethical consideration. By approaching these challenges with clarity, fairness, and open communication, it's possible to create estate plans that honor all family bonds and minimize the risk of costly and painful disputes.

As we strive to stop inheritance heists, let us remember the words of Galatians 6:10: "So then, as we have opportunity, let us do good to everyone, and especially to those who are of the household of faith." In the context of blended families, this calls us to consider the needs and feelings of all family members, striving for solutions that strengthen rather than divide.

In our ongoing mission to stop inheritance heists, understanding the unique challenges faced by blended families is crucial. By recognizing the legal and emotional complexities involved, employing clear communication and detailed planning, and utilizing tools like mediation when conflicts arise, we can help ensure that inheritance becomes a means of honoring family bonds rather than breaking them.

CHAPTER 12
WHEN TRUST BREAKS DOWN: NAVIGATING STEPPARENT INHERITANCE CONFLICTS

In the intricate web of modern family dynamics, few situations are as emotionally charged and potentially devastating as inheritance disputes involving stepparents. This chapter delves into the delicate issue of inheritance heists related to stepparents, with a particular focus on a common scenario that often leads to heartbreaking outcomes for biological children.

THE TYPICAL SCENARIO: A RECIPE FOR CONFLICT

Picture this all-too-common situation:

- An older man marries a younger woman.
- Both spouses have biological children from previous relationships.
- The couple creates an estate plan that appears fair and equitable: a life estate of assets for the surviving spouse; power of invasion of principal by the trustee (usually the surviving spouse); upon the surviving spouse's death, the estate is to be divided equally between all children.

This plan seems reasonable and just. The father of the biological children assumes that his spouse will fulfill their mutual wishes made while they were both alive. However, reality often paints a starkly different picture.

THE COMMON OUTCOME: BETRAYAL OF TRUST

Tragically, the scenario frequently unfolds and defies expectations. We have litigated dozens of these cases and the typical scenario is as follows:

- The wife survives her husband.
- She changes the estate plan to cut out her husband's biological children.
- Using her power of invasion, she takes most of the estate and makes it her separate property, putting it outside the reach of her husband's biological children.
- The husband's biological children often remain unaware of these changes until: they inquire about the trust; or the stepmother dies, and they're informed they'll receive nothing.

The essence of this scenario is a profound betrayal of trust. The father assumed his wishes would be honored, but greed takes over, leaving his children disinherited and often bitter.

THE SCOPE OF THE ISSUE: A GROWING PROBLEM

To understand how widespread this issue potentially is, let's examine some revealing statistics:

- Out of 11.4 million widowed individuals in the United States, 8.9 million are widows (women) and 2.5 million are widowers (men).
- The majority of these widowed individuals are over 65 years old.
- Approximately 30-40% of adults in the United States have at

least one stepparent, a figure that's increasing due to higher divorce and remarriage rates.
- About 40% of married couples with children in the US are step couples, meaning at least one partner has a child from a previous relationship.

These statistics underscore the prevalence of blended families and the potential for inheritance disputes involving stepparents.

THE UNIQUE CHALLENGES OF STEPMOTHER WIDOWS

Stepmothers who are widows face a particularly complex set of challenges that can contribute to the scenario described above:

- Dual Loss: Grappling with the loss of their spouse while navigating the often-tricky waters of stepparenting.
- Blended Family Dynamics: Integrating into an existing family unit while grieving adds layers of complexity.
- Legal Minefields: Inheritance, guardianship, and estate planning can become battlegrounds.
- Emotional Turbulence: Both the widow and the children are dealing with loss, creating a highly charged emotional environment.
- Identity Shifts: Reconciling roles as wives, widows, mothers, and stepmothers.
- Societal Perceptions: Facing misconceptions about motivations and relationships with stepchildren.

HIGH-PROFILE INHERITANCE DISPUTES: WHEN FAMILY CONFLICTS GO PUBLIC

While our typical scenario often plays out in private, high-profile cases can shed light on the potential for conflict. Here are some notable examples:

- The Agee Family Dispute: Involving Mary Cunningham Agee, widow of William M. Agee, former CEO of Bendix Corporation.
- Sol Goldman Family Dispute: A billion-dollar battle over a vast real estate portfolio.
- Peter Falk Estate: A $5 million estate dispute between Falk's widow and his daughter.
- Tom Petty Estate: A $95 million dispute over music catalog and intellectual property rights.
- Alan Thicke Estate: A $15.8 million dispute centered on a California ranch and personal effects.
- Jimi Hendrix Estate: A $175 million dispute over merchandise rights and royalties.
- Anna Nicole Smith/J. Howard Marshall II: A $1.6 billion dispute over oil fortune inheritance.

PREVENTING INHERITANCE HEISTS: STRATEGIES FOR PROTECTION

To avoid these painful and costly disputes, consider the following strategies:

Clear Communication: Openly discuss inheritance plans with all family members, including stepchildren.
Professional Estate Planning: Engage experienced attorneys to create robust, legally sound estate plans.
Regular Updates: Review and update estate plans regularly, especially after major life changes.
Mediation: Consider family mediation to address potential conflicts before they escalate.
Transparency: Maintain clear records and be transparent about financial decisions.
Limited Powers: Consider limiting the surviving spouse's power to change the estate plan or invade the principal.
Separate Trusts: Create separate trusts for biological children to ensure their inheritance is protected.

Co-Trustees: Appoint a co-trustee to oversee the surviving spouse's use of estate assets.

Education: Educate all family members about the estate plan and its intentions to prevent misunderstandings.

CONCLUSION: PRESERVING FAMILY HARMONY AND HONORING WISHES

The intersection of stepfamilies, widowhood, and inheritance is a potential minefield. The typical scenario we've explored – where a surviving stepparent changes the estate plan to benefit their biological children at the expense of their stepchildren – is unfortunately common.

By understanding these dynamics, learning from high-profile disputes, and implementing preventative strategies, families can take proactive steps to prevent their own inheritance heists. Remember, proper estate planning isn't just about distributing assets—it's about preserving family harmony, honoring the wishes of the deceased, and ensuring fairness for all children, biological and step alike.

The key is to address these issues openly and honestly while both partners are alive, and to create legal safeguards that protect the interests of all parties involved. With careful planning, open communication, and a commitment to fairness, blended families can navigate the complex waters of inheritance and emerge with relationships intact.

CHAPTER 13
SAFEGUARDING LEGACIES AND CHAMPIONING JUSTICE

As we conclude our exploration of inheritance heists, it's clear that the landscape of estate litigation is as complex and challenging as ever. From traditional schemes of undue influence and fraud to the new frontiers of cryptocurrency theft and caregiver exploitation, those who seek to subvert the wishes of the deceased are constantly evolving their tactics. Yet, armed with the knowledge and strategies we've discussed throughout this book, we are better equipped than ever to combat these injustices while navigating the emotional complexities inherent in these disputes.

KEY LESSONS AND STRATEGIES

Let's revisit the key lessons we've learned and explore how they can be applied in real-world situations:

Recognizing Inheritance Heists: Inheritance heists come in many forms, from subtle manipulation to outright theft. Vigilance and education are our first lines of defense. For instance, in the case of caregiver exploitation, be alert to signs such as isolation of the elderly person, sudden changes in estate planning documents, or unexplained financial transactions.

Digital Asset Protection: The digital age has brought new challenges, particularly in the realm of cryptocurrency and online assets. As we saw with the O'Sullivan case, proper digital estate planning is crucial. This includes maintaining a secure, up-to-date inventory of digital assets, ensuring proper access protocols, and considering the use of specialized digital estate planning services.

Mediation and Conflict Resolution: Mediation, when skillfully applied, can resolve complex disputes while preserving family relationships. The Johnson family trust mediation demonstrated the power of this approach. Consider engaging a mediator experienced in both estate law and family dynamics to navigate difficult conversations and find mutually acceptable solutions.

Innovative Legal Approaches: Contingency fee arrangements, like those pioneered by Hackard Law, are revolutionizing access to justice in estate litigation. They align the interests of attorneys and clients, ensuring that even those without substantial resources can seek justice. Don't hesitate to explore these options if you find yourself facing a seemingly insurmountable legal challenge.

Trust Distribution and Planning: Trust distribution disasters can be avoided through careful planning and clear communication. When they do occur, swift and decisive legal action is often necessary. Regular family discussions about estate plans, facilitated by a neutral third party if needed, can help prevent misunderstandings and conflicts before they arise.

Combating Caregiver Exploitation: Caregiver exploitation is a significant threat to vulnerable elders. Recognizing the signs of undue influence and implementing safeguards against isolation and financial abuse are crucial. This might include regular family check-ins, professional oversight, and clear documentation of all caregiving and financial arrangements.

Navigating Emotional Complexities: The emotional landscape of inheritance disputes, particularly the role of grief, plays a significant part in how these conflicts unfold and are resolved. Understanding and addressing these emotional aspects is crucial for effective representation and resolution.

Understanding the Presumption of Fraud: The legal concept of presumption of fraud provides a powerful tool for challenging suspicious bequests, particularly those made to caregivers, will drafters, and others in positions of trust. Understanding how this presumption works can be crucial in protecting estates from undue influence and exploitation.

Stepparent Inheritance Dynamics: Recognize the unique challenges posed by stepparent scenarios in inheritance disputes. Be aware of the potential for conflict between surviving spouses and biological children, and implement strategies to prevent these conflicts through clear communication and robust estate planning.

PRACTICAL STRATEGIES FOR EMOTIONAL NAVIGATION

Recognizing the profound impact of emotions on inheritance disputes, consider implementing the following strategies:

Facilitated Family Discussions: Engage a neutral third party to facilitate open dialogues about inheritance plans before conflicts arise. This can help air concerns, clarify intentions, and prevent misunderstandings.

Parallel Counseling: Consider family counseling alongside legal proceedings to address underlying emotional issues. Individual therapy can also help stakeholders process grief, anger, or other complex emotions related to the inheritance conflict.

Self-Care and Stress Management: Emphasize the importance of self-care for all parties involved in prolonged inheritance disputes. This might include regular exercise, mindfulness practices, or maintaining social connections outside of the dispute.

Grief Support: Recognize that inheritance disputes often coincide with the grieving process. Encourage participation in grief support groups or individual grief counseling to help navigate this challenging emotional terrain.

Stepfamily Mediation: In blended family scenarios, consider specialized family mediation that addresses the unique dynamics between stepparents and stepchildren. This can help resolve conflicts and prevent inheritance disputes before they escalate.

REAL-WORLD APPLICATION

To illustrate how these lessons can be applied, consider the hypothetical case of the Johnson family:

The Johnsons, a blended family, are dealing with the estate of Robert Johnson, who recently passed away. His second wife, Sarah, is accused by Robert's adult children of exerting undue influence and mismanaging digital assets. The children are concerned that Sarah might change the estate plan to cut them out entirely. By applying the book's lessons, they:

- Identify potential signs of caregiver exploitation, such as isolation and unusual financial transactions.
- Implement digital asset protection strategies, including hiring a forensic accountant to trace cryptocurrency transactions.
- Engage in mediation to uncover underlying interests and fears, such as Sarah's concern about financial security.
- Balance legal action with efforts to preserve family relationships through family therapy and collaborative projects.

- Investigate whether the presumption of fraud applies to any changes made to Robert's will or trust, particularly those benefiting Sarah or any professional advisors involved in the estate planning process.

FUTURE TRENDS AND PREPAREDNESS

As we look to the future, we must remain vigilant. The methods of potential inheritance heists will continue to evolve, but so too will our strategies to combat them. To stay prepared:

Regular Family Discussions: Schedule annual family meetings to review and update estate plans, adapting to changing circumstances and family dynamics.
Ongoing Education: Stay informed about new forms of assets, such as NFTs or emerging cryptocurrencies, and their implications for estate planning. Learn about evolving exploitation techniques, particularly those targeting digital assets or vulnerable elders.
Embrace Technological Solutions: Explore digital tools for secure storage and transfer of estate planning documents.
Legal Developments: Stay informed about changes in estate law, particularly regarding the presumption of fraud and undue influence. As case law evolves, so too may the application and interpretation of these legal concepts.

INTERDISCIPLINARY APPROACH

Addressing inheritance disputes effectively often requires a team of professionals working in concert:

Financial Advisors: Engage them to provide a clear picture of the estate's assets and liabilities and create financial plans that can prevent disputes.
Mental Health Professionals: Involve geriatric psychiatrists to assess mental capacity and family therapists to facilitate improved communication.

Elder Care Specialists: Consult with geriatric care managers to ensure proper care for elderly family members, reducing the risk of caregiver exploitation.
Digital Asset Experts: Collaborate with IT professionals who specialize in digital estate planning and cybersecurity.
Collaborative Law Approach: Consider using a team of professionals (lawyers, financial advisors, mental health professionals) to resolve disputes without going to court.
Estate Planning Attorneys: Consult with estate planning specialists who understand the nuances of the presumption of fraud to ensure that estate plans are structured in ways that can withstand potential challenges.
Family Dynamics Experts: Engage professionals who specialize in blended family dynamics to help navigate the complex relationships and potential conflicts in stepparent inheritance scenarios.

A CALL TO ACTION

To those who may be facing an inheritance dispute, remember that you are not alone. Seek out knowledgeable legal counsel, be proactive in understanding your rights, and don't be afraid to stand up for what's right. At the same time, recognize that you may be navigating complex emotions, including grief. Don't hesitate to seek emotional support alongside legal guidance.

For those involved in estate planning, let this book serve as a call to action. Regular reviews and updates of your estate plan, clear communication with your heirs, and thoughtful consideration of digital assets can go a long way in preventing future disputes. Consider not just the financial aspects of your legacy, but also the emotional impact your decisions may have on your loved ones.

THE PATH FORWARD

As we close this book, let us remember that at the heart of every inheritance is a legacy -- not just of wealth, but of values, memories, and familial bonds. When we fight against inheritance heists, we're not just protecting material assets; we're honoring the wishes of those who came before us and preserving the foundations of family unity for generations to come.

In my nearly five decades of legal practice, I've seen the devastating impact of inheritance heists, but I've also witnessed the triumph of justice and the power of the law to right wrongs. I've learned the importance of balancing legal expertise with emotional intelligence, recognizing that behind every case is a human story of loss, grief, and hope.

At Hackard Law, we remain committed to this fight, standing ready to champion the rights of rightful heirs and beneficiaries across California. We approach each case with a deep understanding of both the legal complexities and the emotional nuances involved, striving to provide representation that addresses both the practical and personal aspects of inheritance disputes.

It's encouraging to see increased focus from prosecutors on cases of elder financial abuse and caregiver exploitation. This sends a strong message that such actions will not be tolerated by society or the legal system. At the same time, we must continue to advocate for resources and support for families navigating the emotional challenges of inheritance disputes.

The battle against inheritance heists is ongoing, but armed with knowledge, vigilance, and the right legal support, it's a battle we can win. Moreover, by approaching these conflicts with empathy and understanding, we can hope to resolve disputes in ways that not only serve justice but also promote healing and reconciliation within families.

Whether we're leveraging the presumption of fraud to challenge suspicious bequests or defending against such claims, our goal remains the same: to ensure that the true intentions of the deceased are honored and protected. The presumption of fraud, like many of the tools we've discussed, is a powerful instrument in our arsenal against inheritance heists. When wielded with skill and compassion, it can be a force for justice, helping to ensure that vulnerability is not exploited for personal gain.

Together, we can ensure that legacies are protected, families are preserved, vulnerable elders are safeguarded, and justice is served. In doing so, we honor not just the letter of the law, but the spirit of love and care that underlies every well-intentioned inheritance. Let us move forward with determination, compassion, and hope, ready to face the challenges of inheritance disputes with wisdom, strength, and unity.

GLOSSARY OF TERMS

Ademption: The failure of a specific bequest due to the gifted property no longer being part of the estate at the time of the testator's death.

Administrator: A person appointed by the court to manage and distribute the estate of someone who died without a will (intestate). This role is similar to that of an executor, but for intestate estates.

Adult Protective Services (APS): A social services program provided by state and local governments serving older adults and adults with disabilities who are in need of assistance.

Anosognosia: A condition common in dementia where individuals are unaware of their own cognitive impairment. This can complicate estate planning and increase vulnerability to exploitation.

BATNA: Best Alternative to a Negotiated Agreement, a concept used in negotiation theory.

Beneficiary: A person or entity entitled to receive benefits from a trust or estate.

Best Alternative to a Negotiated Agreement (BATNA): The most favorable option available if negotiations fail.

Blended Family: A family unit where one or both parents have children from previous relationships, often including children they've had together.

Blended Family Trust: A trust specifically designed to address the unique needs and potential conflicts in families with stepchildren or half-siblings.

Blockchain: A decentralized, digital ledger technology that records transactions across many computers, often used in cryptocurrency systems. Understanding blockchain is crucial for managing digital assets in estates.

Breach of Fiduciary Duty: Failure to act in the best interests of another party when obligated to do so, often in the context of managing assets or estates.

Capacity: The mental ability to understand and make rational decisions about one's affairs, particularly in the context of estate planning. Legal capacity is a crucial factor in determining the validity of wills and trusts.

Care Custodian: In legal terms, typically defined as someone who provides health or social services to a dependent adult.

Caregiver: A person who provides assistance with daily living activities to an individual who cannot fully care for themselves due to age, illness, or disability.

Caregiver Isolation: A tactic used by exploitative caregivers to separate elders from their family and friends, increasing the elder's dependence on the caregiver and making exploitation easier.

Codicil: A legal document that modifies an existing will.

Cold Storage: A method of keeping cryptocurrency offline to reduce the risk of hacking or theft. Important for securing digital assets in estate planning.

Conservatorship: A legal arrangement where a court appoints a person to manage the financial affairs and/or daily life of another due to physical or mental limitations.

Contestable Transaction: A financial transaction or transfer of assets that may be legally challenged due to suspicions of undue influence, lack of capacity, or fraud.

Contingency Fee: A fee arrangement where the attorney only gets paid if they win the case, with the payment coming as a percentage of the winnings.

Cryptocurrency: A type of digital or virtual currency that uses cryptography for security, making it difficult to counterfeit. It operates independently of a central bank and uses blockchain technology. Examples include Bitcoin and Ethereum.

Cy pres doctrine: A legal principle that allows a court to interpret the terms of a charitable trust to fulfill its purpose as closely as possible when the original purpose becomes impossible or impracticable.

Digital Assets: Any content, files, or accounts owned by an individual that exist in digital form, either online or on digital devices. This includes social media accounts, online banking, digital photos, and email accounts.

Digital Estate Plan: A plan that specifically addresses the management and distribution of digital assets after death.

Discretionary trust: A trust where the trustee has discretion over when and how to distribute assets to beneficiaries.

Dunning-Kruger Effect: A cognitive bias where individuals with low ability overestimate their competence. This can affect how individuals perceive their own capacity to manage complex estate matters.

Durable Power of Attorney: A legal document that remains in effect if the principal becomes incapacitated, allowing the appointed agent to make decisions on their behalf.

Elder Abuse: Any act which causes harm to an older person and is carried out by someone they know and trust, such as a family member or friend. The abuse may be physical, social, financial, psychological or sexual and can include mistreatment and neglect.

Elder Financial Abuse: The illegal or improper use of an elder's funds, property, or assets.

Elder Law: A legal specialty focused on issues affecting older adults, including estate planning, long-term care, and elder abuse.

Elective share: The portion of a deceased spouse's estate that a surviving spouse is entitled to claim in lieu of what they would receive under the will.

Estate: The total of all possessions owned by an individual at the time of their death, including real estate, personal property, investments, and other assets.

Estate Freeze: A strategy used to limit the growth of an estate's value for tax purposes, often used in family business succession planning.

Estate Planning: The process of arranging for the management and disposal of a person's estate during their life and after death, including the creation of wills, trusts, and other legal documents to ensure one's wishes are carried out.

Estate Tax: A tax levied on the transfer of a deceased person's estate, typically based on the total value of the assets, as opposed to an inheritance tax which is levied on the recipients of an inheritance.

Executor: A person or entity appointed in a will to administer the estate of the deceased, including managing assets, paying debts and taxes, and distributing property to beneficiaries.

Fiduciary: A person or entity that has a legal and ethical relationship of trust with another party and is obligated to act in their best interests.

Fiduciary Duty: A legal obligation of a person or entity to act in the best interests of another party. Trustees have a fiduciary duty to the beneficiaries of the trust.

Filial Piety: A concept in some cultures emphasizing respect, obedience, and care for one's parents and elders. This can influence inheritance expectations and disputes, especially in multicultural contexts.

Financial Elder Abuse: The illegal or improper use of an elderly person's funds, property, or assets. See also: Elder Abuse

Forensic Accounting: The use of accounting skills to investigate financial records, often used in inheritance dispute cases to trace assets or uncover financial abuse.

Freeze Out: A tactic used in inheritance disputes where one party systematically isolates an elder from their family and friends, often as a precursor to financial exploitation.

Genogram: A pictorial display of a family's relationships, often used in family therapy and mediation to understand complex family dynamics in inheritance disputes.

Guardianship: A legal relationship created when a court appoints an individual to care for a minor child or incapacitated adult.

Hardware Wallet: A physical device used to store cryptocurrency offline, providing enhanced security for digital assets. Also known as a cold wallet, it's not connected to the internet, reducing the risk of hacking.

Holographic will: A will that is handwritten by the testator.

Inheritance: Property or assets received from someone who has died.

Inheritance Tax: A tax imposed on individuals who receive property from the estate of a deceased person.

Intestate: The state of dying without a valid will, resulting in the distribution of assets according to state law rather than the deceased's wishes.

Intestate Succession: The process by which a deceased person's assets are distributed when they die without a valid will.

Life Estate: A type of property ownership where a person has the right to use and occupy a property during their lifetime, but does not have the right to sell or transfer the property after their death. Often used in estate planning for blended families.

Living Trust: A trust created during a person's lifetime, allowing them to maintain control of their assets while alive, with a successor trustee taking over management upon death or incapacity.

Mediation: A process of alternative dispute resolution where a neutral third party (mediator) helps conflicting parties reach a mutually acceptable solution.

No-Contest Clause: A provision in a will or trust that threatens to disinherit beneficiaries who challenge the document.

Non-Fungible Token (NFT): A unique digital asset stored on a blockchain, representing ownership of a specific item or piece of content. NFTs are becoming increasingly relevant in digital estate planning.

Perjury: The act of willfully telling an untruth in a court after having taken an oath or affirmation.

Pet Trust: A legal arrangement that provides for the care and maintenance of one or more pets in the event of the owner's disability or death. This type of trust is becoming more common in estate planning.

Pour-Over Will: A will that transfers any assets not already in a trust into that trust upon the person's death.

Power of Appointment: A provision in a trust or will that allows a designated individual to determine how certain assets should be distributed. For example, a trust grantor might give their spouse the power to decide how to distribute assets among their children.

Power of Attorney: A legal document giving one person (the agent) the power to act for another person (the principal).

Presumption of Fraud: A legal presumption that certain transactions, particularly those involving vulnerable individuals or those in positions of trust, are fraudulent unless proven otherwise.

Probate: The legal process of administering a deceased person's estate, including validating the will, paying debts, and distributing assets to beneficiaries.

Probate Court: A specialized court that handles matters related to the administration of estates, including the validation of wills, appointment of executors, and resolution of estate disputes.

Prudent Investor Rule: A legal standard requiring a trustee to invest trust assets as a prudent investor would, considering the purposes, terms, distribution requirements, and other circumstances of the trust.

QTIP Trust: Qualified Terminable Interest Property Trust, a type of trust that allows a grantor to provide for a surviving spouse and maintain control of how the trust's assets are distributed once the surviving spouse dies.

Reservation Value: The least favorable point at which one will accept a negotiated agreement. It's the point beyond which you would walk away from a negotiation.

Seed Phrase: A series of words used to access and recover cryptocurrency wallets.

Settlor: The person who creates a trust, also known as the grantor or trustor.

Spendthrift clause: A provision in a trust that prevents beneficiaries from transferring their interest in the trust and protects the trust from creditors.

Statute of Limitations: The time limit within which legal action must be initiated in estate-related matters, such as contesting a will or claiming inheritance.

Step-up Basis: A readjustment of the value of an appreciated asset for tax purposes upon inheritance. The asset receives a new basis equal to its fair market value on the date of the previous owner's death, potentially reducing capital gains tax liability for the heir.

Successor Trustee: The person or entity named to take over the management of a trust when the original trustee is unable or unwilling to serve.

Tangible Personal Property: Physical items that can be moved, such as furniture, jewelry, or vehicles, as opposed to real estate or intangible assets like digital property.

Testamentary Capacity: The specific mental capacity required to make or change a valid will and/or trust.

Testator: The person who makes and executes a will. This term is crucial in discussions of will validity and interpretation.

Trust: A legal arrangement where one party (the trustee) holds assets on behalf of another party (the beneficiary).

Trust Distribution: The process of allocating assets from a trust to its beneficiaries according to the trust's terms.

Trustee: The person who manages a trust according to its terms and in the best interest of the beneficiaries. See also: Fiduciary Duty

Two-Factor Authentication: A security process in which the user provides two different authentication factors to verify their identity, often used to secure digital accounts and assets.

Undue Influence: Improper pressure exerted on a person to make decisions they wouldn't otherwise make, often in the context of changing a will or trust. Often a grounds for contesting a will or trust.

Worst Alternative to a Negotiated Agreement (WATNA): The least favorable option available if negotiations fail.

Will: A legal document that specifies how a person's assets should be distributed after their death.

Zone of Possible Agreement (ZOPA): The range between each party's reservation value within which an agreement is possible in a negotiation.

INDEX

A

Abraham's Mourning 38
Absalom 37
Absolute skepticism 25
Acceptance 36
Acknowledge the Pain 38
Active Listening 59, 61, 66
Adapting the Blueprint 17
Administrator 25, 97-98, 100-101, 127
Adult abuse 81
Adult Protective Services (APS) 81, 127
Alan Thicke Estate 116
Albert Lawson 8
Altcoins 96
Altered documents 48
Alternative dispute resolution 14-15, 51, 131
Alzheimer's disease 88
Amended pleadings 49
American Bar Association 4, 45
Anger 35, 55, 59, 69, 86, 120
Anger Management 69
Anosognosia 127

INDEX

Asking Probing Questions 61
Assessing Your BATNA 60
Attorney-Client Relationship 47
Avoiding Coercion 64

B

Background checks 92
Balancing Power Dynamics 64
Balancing Security 103
Bankrupt Beneficiary 12
Barbara Stokely 77, 80
Bendix Corporation 116
Beneficiary 7, 12, 22, 33, 93, 106, 108, 127, 133
Bible 26, 37, 43, 105
Biological children 113-114, 116-117, 120
Bitcoin (BTC) 96
Blended families 18, 104-105, 110-112, 115, 117, 131
Blended Family Dynamics 115, 123
Blended Family Trust 127
Blind Bidding 64
Blockchain 96, 102, 128-129, 131
BMO Wealth Management 4
Breach of Fiduciary Duty 101, 109, 128
Brian Geremia 101
Broken relationships 51

C

California Probate Code 25, 53
Capacity Issues 70
Care Custodian 82, 128
Caregiver 10, 41, 54, 56, 81-94, 118-119, 121, 123-124, 128
Caregiver Capers 81, 93
Caregiver exploitation 41, 81-83, 87-89, 91-92, 94, 118-119, 121, 123-124
Caregiver Isolation 128
Caregiver's Windfall 54

Caring.com 4
Carlos Martinez 49, 106
Certificate of Independent Review 55
Changing the Game 24, 63
Checklist for Trust Creators 15
Chess Game of Mediation 61
Choosing the right trustee 14
Clear and specific trust language 13, 18
Clear communication 10, 15, 31, 56, 68, 80, 108-110, 112, 116, 119-120, 123
Clear documentation 91, 119
Clear Succession Planning 102
Codicil 128
Cognitive decline 20, 22
Cognitive Impairment 55, 76, 85, 127
Cold Storage 96, 128
Collaborative Law Approach 123
Communication protocols 31
Communication style 40
Competing Spousal Rights 109
Complex family structures 105
Conflict Avoidance 68
Conflict Resolution 67, 119
Conservatorship 92, 128
Consumer Attorneys of California (CAOC) 27
Consumer Attorneys of California (CAOC) 27
Contestable Transaction 128
Contingency Fee 24, 27-33, 119, 128
Contingency fee model 24, 27, 30, 33
Contingent Agreements 64
Co-Trustees 117
Creative Solutions 60, 77, 80, 111
Criminal charges 49-50, 92
Criminal prosecution 50, 92
Cross-Cultural Factors 68
Cryptocurrency 12, 24, 59, 95-103, 118-119, 121, 128, 130, 132

Cryptocurrency Litigation 95

D

Dave Jones 101
Dependent Adult Civil Protection Act 92
Depression 36
Desire for Connection 85
Digital Asset Division 70
Digital Asset Experts 123
Digital Asset Inventory 102
Digital Asset Protection 119, 121
Digital assets 70, 96-97, 99, 101-103, 119, 121-123, 128-130
Digital estate planning 102, 119, 123, 131
Digital evidence 30
Digital footprints 102
Digital forensics 101
Digital landscape 103
Discretionary trust 129
Donative transfer 53
Door in the Face 62
Double-Edged Sword of Dishonesty 42
Dr. Elena Rodriguez 78
Dunning-Kruger Effect 129
Durable Power of Attorney 129

E

Educate clients 51
Education 13, 79, 87, 91, 102, 106, 117-118, 122
Elder Abuse 39, 41, 81, 92-93, 101, 109, 129-130
Elder Abuse 92
Elder Abuse and Dependent Adult Civil Protection Act 92
Elder Abuse Litigation 92
Elder Care Specialists 123
Elder Financial Abuse 7, 124, 129
Elective share 129
Emotional Preparation 56

Emotional toll 12, 51, 55-56
Emotional Turbulence 115
Emotional Volatility 62
Empathetic Listening 36
Encourage communication 51
Encourage Support Systems 39
Encrypted files 100
Enforceability 65, 70
Enforcement prosecution 101
Estate and trust litigation 24-25, 27-28, 30, 33, 35
Estate disputes 11, 33, 75, 79, 102, 132
Estate planning 4, 7-9, 13, 15, 17-22, 25, 30, 79-80, 83-84, 90-91, 95, 99, 102-104, 109-110, 112, 115-120, 122-123, 127-131
Estate Planning Attorneys 13, 22, 123
Estate planning safeguards 91
Estate Tax 99, 130
Ethereum (ETH) 96
Ethical Dilemma for Attorneys 45
European-American Traditions 67
Evaluating the ZOPA 60
Evelyn Janssen 75-76
Existing Estate Plans 70
Exodus 20:16 43
Expanding the pie 66
Extended Family Involvement 67
Extraordinary services 25

F

Fabricated debts 48
Facebook 95
False accusations 48
Familismo 68
Family dynamics 8-10, 13-14, 20, 22, 33, 57-58, 60, 69, 80, 110-111, 113, 115, 119, 122-123, 130
Family Involvement 67, 87
Fear of loss 44

Fear of rejection by legal counsel 44
Fee shifting 49
Fiduciary duty 101, 109-110, 128, 130, 133
Fiduciary Duty Conflicts 110
Filial Piety 8, 67, 130
Financial Advisors 122-123
Financial audits 49
Financial Control 84
Financial Elder Abuse 92, 101, 109, 130
Financial exploitation 81, 85, 89-91, 93, 130
Financial Safeguards 87
Financial transactions 14, 49, 90-91, 118, 121
Financial Vulnerability 85
Flexibility is key 21
Forensic accountants 29-30, 93
Forensic accountants 29-30, 93
Forensic Accounting 109, 130
Forensic analysis 48
Forensic financial investigation 108
Forgotten Sibling 12
Fraudulent Conveyance 101
Freeze Out 88, 130

G

Gabriel Case 5
Generational Differences 68
Genogram 130
Geriatric psychiatrists 93, 122
Gonzales Family Dilemma 88
Google 95
Grief counseling 36-37, 40, 56, 63, 69, 87, 121
Grief Counseling Techniques 69
Grief Support 121

H

Hackard Law 7, 9, 24, 27, 29-30, 33-34, 49, 77, 92-93, 100-101, 109, 119, 124
Handwritten will 76, 78-79
Hardware wallets 96-97
Harold and Vivian Case 107
Heidi Miller 90
Helpful Nephew 54
Hidden assets 30, 48-49, 101
High-profile inheritance disputes 115
Holographic will 131
Hon. Ed Greene (Ret.) 65
Hourly rates 25-26
Hypothetical Future Scenarios 64

I

Implementation Plan 65
Increased legal costs 51
Increased longevity 20
Independent Administration of Estates Act 98
Individualism vs. Family Legacy 67
Inheritanc Tax 130-131
Inheritance Disputes 17, 20-21, 24, 33, 35, 38-39, 41-42, 48-53, 55-60, 62-63, 67, 69, 71, 80, 91, 103-104, 106-109, 111, 113, 115, 120-122, 124-125, 130
Inheritance Dynamics 120
Inheritance heist 94
Innovative Legal Approaches 119
Intestacy 4
Intestate Succession 131

J

Jesus at Lazarus's Tomb 38
Jimi Hendrix Estate 116
Job's Grief 37
Joyce Mahoney 91

Judeo-Christian ethics 26, 43

L

Labeling Concessions 61
Language Barriers 68
Lawson family's story 14
Lawson Inheritance 7-9
Legal capacity 128
Legal Landscape 53
Legal Minefields 115
Legal presumption 53-54, 132
Legal System Trust 68
LexisNexis 4
Life estate 113, 131
Life Insurance 6-7, 110
Lifetime trust 19
Loss of inheritance 51

M

Mandatory income payments 18
Maria Rodriguez 29
Mariana Batista 91
Martinez Estate 49
Martinez-Thompson case 105, 109-111
Martinez-Thompson Case 105, 109-111
Mediated settlement agreement 70
Mediation as a tool 10
Melissa Thompson 83
Mental Health Professionals 37, 122-123
Mental Health Support 37
Missing Cryptocurrencies 101
Model Rules of Professional Conduct 45
Motions for sanctions 49
Mysterious Transfers 100

N

Nancy White 17
Nancy's Legacy 17, 22
National Association of Estate Planners & Councils 4
National Council on Aging 81
New Jersey 6
NFTs 96, 122, 131
No-Contest Clause 131
Nuclear Family Focus 67

O

Odalis Lopez 90
Online Collaboration Tools 70
Online Dispute Resolution (ODR) 70
Open communication 7, 11, 14, 20, 23, 59, 69, 92, 112, 117
Oral Traditions 68

P

Parallel Counseling 120
Partial Distributions 100
Pat O'Brien 100-101
Perjury charges 49
Peter Falk Estate 116
Pew Research Center 104
Policy Advocacy 33
Pour-Over Will 131
Power of appointment 19, 131
Power of Attorney Limitations 89
Presumption of fraud 53-57, 120, 122-124
Presumption of fraud 53-57, 120, 122-124, 132
Principal distributions 18
Privacy 5, 7, 49, 75, 82, 84, 96, 99, 106, 111
Probate Code § 21362 82
Probate Code 22, 25, 53, 82
Probate Code sections 10800 and 10810 25
Probate court 98, 100-101, 106, 132

Probate process 5
Professional Boundaries 37
Professional Fiduciaries 89
Professional Oversight 10, 15, 87, 91, 94, 119
Promote Healing 39, 124

Q

QTIP trust 110, 132
Qualified Terminable Interest Property (QTIP) 110
Questions to Ask Your Estate Planning Attorney 15
Quran 37

R

Reckless Investor Trustee 12
Reflective Listening 62
Regular Accounting 90
Regular Check-ins 87
Regular Family Check-ins 91, 94, 119
Regular trust reviews and updates 13
Reputation damage 51
Respecting Confidentiality 64
Revenge 42, 44
Revolutionizing Access to Justice in Inheritance Disputes 24
Risk Sharing 27
Robert O'Sullivan 95
Rodriguez Family 29
Rodriguez Family Trust Dispute 29
Role of Legal Counsel 21

S

Sale of Family Assets 107
Sam Collins 100-101
San Francisco 29
San Jose 75, 107
Sanctions 49-50
Sarah Jensen 82, 84

Sarah Jensen Case 82, 84
Senator Hiram Johnson 42
Separate trusts for each child 18
Set clear expectations 51
Sibling Showdowns 5
Skilled mediator 60, 111
Societal Perceptions 115
Sol Goldman 116
Spendthrift clause 132
Statute of Limitations 132
Statutory fees 25
Stepfamily Mediation 121
Stephany Hernandez 90
Steven White 18
Steven's Dilemma 18
Sudden Wealth 100
Susan Thompson 106

T

Tangible Personal Property 133
Tax Implications 15, 70
Technological Integration 33
Testamentary Capacity 133
Thessalonians 38
Thomas 8-9
Thorough discovery 48
Timing 12, 36, 47
Tom Petty Estate 116
Torah 37
Trust contests 92
Trust Distribution 3, 5, 11, 13-15, 17-18, 119, 133
Trust distribution disasters 3, 11, 13-15, 18, 119
Trust Modification 20-21, 107
Trustee mismanagement 12
Truth About Lies 42
Twitter 95

Two-factor authentication 97, 133
Tyler 75-76, 78-79

U

Understanding the stages of grief 35
Undisclosed Assets 100
Undue influence 7, 9, 12, 29, 48-49, 53-55, 83-86, 88, 91-94, 108-109, 118-122, 128, 133
Undue Influence Claims 92, 109
Unknown passwords 97
Unmasking deception 33, 48
Urinary tract infection (UTI) 76
Use Caucuses Effectively 62

V

Validate Emotions 39
Validation 36, 132
Valuation of Non-Liquid Assets 30
Verbal agreements 68
Video Conferencing 70
Visitation Rights 90
Vivian 107-108
Vulnerable elders 81, 87, 90-91, 119, 122, 125

W

White Family 17, 19-23, 61, 92
William M. Agee 116
Witness interviews 49, 109
Worst Alternative to a Negotiated Agreement (WATNA) 133

Z

Zealous advocacy 47
Zone of Possible Agreement (ZOPA) 133

ABOUT THE AUTHOR

Michael Hackard, Esq., is the founder of Hackard Law, a California law firm focused on several areas of law, including representing victims of traumatic brain injury (TBI). He practiced law for over 45 years before writing *Inheritance Heists* and has been interviewed regularly by local and national media, including *The Wall Street Journal*, CSPAN and Fox News, and has testified before the U.S. House of Representatives.

ALSO BY MICHAEL HACKARD

Michael has also written the books *The Wolf at the Door: Undue Influence and Elder Financial Abuse* and *Alzheimer's, Widowed Stepmothers & Estate Crimes: Cause, Action, and Response in Cases of Fractured Inheritance, Lost Inheritance, and Disinheritance.*

www.ingramcontent.com/pod-product-compliance
Lightning Source LLC
Chambersburg PA
CBHW030438010526
44118CB00011B/686